D1218304

Modern Brazilian Poetry

Indiana University Press
Bloomington / 1 9 6 2

MODERN

BRAZILIAN POETRY

AN ANTHOLOGY

translated and edited, with the help of Yolanda Leite, by

JOHN NIST

Reprinted with the permission of the original publisher
KRAUS REPRINT CORPORATION
New York
1968

ACKNOWLEDGEMENT is made to the following quarterly journals for permission to reprint the poems listed: *Beliot Poetry Journal* (Fall 1959), Manuel Bandeira's "Poetica," Pneumothorax," "Absolute Death," "Apple," "Roundel of the Little Horses," "I Am Going Away to Pasargada," and "Last Song of the Dead End"; Cecilia Meireles' "Introduction," "Portrait," "Motive," "Guitar," "The Roosters Will Crow," "Pastoral," "Museum," "The Archangel," and "The Gates of Midnight"; and Carlos Drummond de Andrade's "Pathetic Poem," "Secret," "The Dirty Hand," "Sadness in Heaven," "The Ox," "Search for Poetry," "Dawn," and "Aspiration"; *Approach* (Fall 1959), Manuel Bandeira's "Profundamente"; *Arizona Quarterly* (Winter 1960), Mario de Andrade's "Song of the Corner," and Vinicius de Morais' "Christmas Poem"; *New Mexico Quarterly Review* (Summer 1960), Vinicius de Morais' "Epitaph"; *The DePauw Magazine* (Winter 1960-61), Paul Bomfim's "Tempest," "Madness," and "Hands." The Introduction is adapted from the first half of the article "Modern Brazilian Literature: A Panorama," which appeared in the Winter, 1960 issue of *Arizona Quarterly*.

Printed in U.S.A.

FOR
ALL MY MANY BRAZILIAN FRIENDS
com um abraço bem apertado

CONTENTS

INTRODUCTION

It is highly doubtful that poets have ever assumed the exalted role which an exuberant (at times hysterical) Percy Bysshe Shelley claimed for them. But if poets are scarcely "the unacknowledged legislators of the world," in Brazil, at least, they are the prophetic avant-garde of all the arts. In Brazil, Modernism began as a formal artistic force one wild week in 1922, in the Municipal Theater of São Paulo. Mario de Andrade (1893–1945), both Paraclete and Exegete of the new movement, led an open revolt against the satisfied and well-entrenched tradition of the Parnassians. This tradition had exhausted itself by becoming fawningly imitative of the Portuguese, rigidly grammatical, too technically "correct." Neither native nor idiomatic, far removed from the interests of the Brazilian people, Parnassian poetry was suffocating under the heavy blankets of Hellenism and modern French and Italian influences. Together with Oswald de Andrade (1890–1954), founder of *Revista de Antropofagia (Review of Cannibalism)*, Mario championed a return to Brazil's heroic past, revived interest in the sublime sculpturing of Antonio Francisco Lisboa (1730–1814), fostered a growing desire to portray the problems of Brazil's Negroes, her poor and depressed, and provided an electric impulse to the other arts. Thus Villa-Lobos, Brazil's leading musician, and Portinari, her outstanding painter, owe much of their success and lasting strength to the new vision of life and art that was liberated in the writing of Mario and Oswald de Andrade (same last name, but not related).

Despite the fact that Brazil's greatest writer is the short-story teller and novelist Machado de Assis (1839–1908), despite the fact that her greatest single book is probably the prose epic *Rebellion In The Backlands (Os Sertões,* 1902) by Euclides da Cunha (1866–1909), the leading genre of literary achievement in Brazil has been poetry. And ever since 1922 Brazilian poets have blazed the way, followed, in order of their appearance and value, by the novelists, the short-story writers, and the dramatists.

The first phase of Modern Brazilian poetry, running approximately from 1920 to 1930, is marked by humor, dry wit, irony, and satire. In their violent reaction against the Parnassians, Mario and Oswald were joined by Guilherme de Almeida (b. 1890) and Cassiano Ricardo (b. 1895). These four poets sought to mystify, to shock the bourgeois. In order to accomplish their desire to write boldly, to enlarge the sensibility of their age, they sought to destroy the old language. Gay, lionized by the chic cocktail-party set of São Paulo, Oswald de Andrade, for example, accepted typographical mistakes as permanent changes in his texts: droll and delicious, these mistakes furthered the cause of fattening a too-long lean and hungry sense of humor. Mario de Andrade, on the other hand, reveled in the use of startling imagery, mental and syntactical ellipses, violent juxtapositions of romantic sentiment and earthy reality, ironic twists, and irreverent laughter.

The first phase of Modernism in Brazilian poetry was something like the Jazz Age in the United States: with the coming of the Great Depression, much of the champagne laughter stopped. The second phase of Modernism in Brazil began in 1930. The poets continued to be sensitive to the times, but the new moderns were more serious. Manuel Bandeira (b. 1886), the most important poet of the first phase of Modernism, still longed, however, for the absolute freedom of his mythic Paradise —Pasargada. Bandeira, now secretary of the august Brazilian Academy of Letters, also distilled the quintessence of the artistic revolution into one statement of supreme disgust in "Poetica." Yet despite his eloquent warning in favor of inspiration over technique (a warning that might very well be heeded by American poets), the second phase of Brazilian Modernism produced a return to preoccupation with perfection of form—an interest which continues even in prose to this very day.

Two main trends obtain in this second phase: 1. the sociopolitical and 2. the religio-mystical. The first trend is marked by a movement to the left, by a concern for the underdog, by a belief in the achievement of a better world and in the ending of social injustice. As a literary movement, this trend emphasizes the brotherhood of man; it is a form of sentimental optimism, seeking organization in either Communism or Socialism. The high priest of this trend in Brazil is undoubtedly Carlos Drummond de Andrade (b. 1902). A great poet by any critical standard, Carlos Drummond has recently become disenchanted with his earlier political beliefs, but he has never abandoned his love affair with poetry—poetry that is intellectually tough, emotionally sympathetic, ironic, and technically perfect.

The religio-mystical trend of this second phase emphasized a kind of faith without God; it too continued the interest in perfection of form. The three outstanding poets of this trend are Murilo Mendes (b. 1902), Augusto Frederico Schmidt (b. 1906), and Cecilia Meireles (b. 1901). Under the influence of Freudian psychology, Mendes wrote a surrealistic poetry of metaphysical depth. Schmidt (today a wealthy industrialist and powerful politician) made a personal pilgrimage back to the versicles of the Bible and the oceanic rhythms of Whitman to find a proper vehicle for his prophecies. Cecilia Meireles, the finest woman poet in the Portuguese language, looked to nature, Brazil's heroic past, and the European Middle Ages for her subject matter. Perhaps the most purely lyrical of all Brazil's fine modern poets, Cecilia Meireles achieves a kind of simple word magic that results in asthetic hypnosis; she is a true disciple of John Keats at his mature best.

The third phase of Brazilian Modernism commenced around 1940; younger poets began to turn away from several of the ism's: regional, nature, humor, social, and political. They became even more concerned with form, with rhythms and words. Under the influence of T. S. Eliot and the New Criticism in America, these younger Brazilian poets began to follow Cecilia Meireles (not in subject matter) into an aestheticism that demanded pure poetry as its proper outlet. Clinging fast to the new language wrought for them by Mario de Andrade and Manuel Bandeira, they nevertheless wanted to pour this new wine into the old bottles of classical control. Fascinated with the possibilities of Imagism, these poets of the third phase sought to make their works highly metaphorical. Though contemporary with the giants of the first phase, Jorge de Lima (1893–1953), the most versatile of all modern Brazilian poets, moved through academic revolt, regionalism, and the religio-mystical trend of the second phase (he wanted "to reconstitute poetry in Christ") to inspired symbolic poems of personal anguish. His youngest peers in this phase are Vinicius de Morais (b. 1913), government diplomat, whose emotional power and stylistic virtuosity are undisputed, and Domingos Carvalho da Silva (b. 1915), critic-journalist for *Diario de São Paulo* and compassionate craftsman par excellence.

By 1950 the influences of Ezra Pound and e. e. cummings, of Swiss Concretism and the calligrammes of Apollinaire were being felt in Brazil. With these newly released energies, the fourth phase of Brazilian Modernism sought to turn a temporal art into a spacial. Many young Brazilian poets of this fourth phase want to disintegrate the word into sight-pattern elements in order to achieve the beauty of a concrete object. Their battle cry is "A poem is a *graphic* thing." Extremely vocal, the Concretists and Neo-Concretists carry on their aesthetic debates in the *Journal of Brazil*·in Rio de Janeiro, influence contemporary painting and sculpture to assume their principles, and cry for their new poetry to appear as murals in the new capital: Brasilia. Many older poets and critics, however, feel that too much confusion over principles vitiates the achievements of these new poets. The outstanding Concretists are Ferreira Gular, Augusto de Campos, and Decio Pignatari. Yet despite the vociferations of the Concretists, the greatest Brazilian poet of their generation is probably João Cabral de Melo Neto (b. 1920). João Cabral brings a profoundly symbolic mind to bear upon his experimentations; it is the very quality of his intellect that saves him from being carried away by a naive enthusiasm for the achievements of the intellect per se. Among the younger poets writing in Brazil today, perhaps the most promising is Paulo Bomfim (b. 1927), actor and star on radio and television, who won an award from the Brazilian Academy of Letters when he was nineteen.

Meanwhile, the older established poets continue to create. Cassiano Ricardo, for example, has matured into a great psychological poet. Together with a consuming interest in his own personal ugliness, Ricardo is now appropriating modern scientific advances as subject matter for his most recent poems. Cecilia Meireles is busy working with classical limpidity upon mystical and Romantic themes. Carlos Drummond de Andrade is singing simple lyrics and tales for his grandchildren. Vinicius de Morais, author of *Orfeu Negro*, winner of the Gold Medal at the 1959 Cannes Film Festival, is moving on into verse drama. But regardless of their subject or approach, these four poets are the masters of their contemporaries and, in turn, of their disciples. If one were forced to select the outstanding dozen modern poets of Brazil, his final list would have to read something like this: Manuel Bandeira, Mario de Andrade, Jorge de Lima, Cassiano Ricardo, Cecilia Meireles, Carlos Drummond de Andrade, Murilo Mendes, Augusto Frederico Schmidt, Vinicius de Morais, Domingos Carvalho da Silva, João Cabral de Melo Neto, and Paulo Bomfim—the twelve poets, in short, who constitute this present anthology. Authorities on Brazilian literature may wish to quarrel with one or two choices on the list, but taken as a whole, it, I think, is firm and secure.

In São Paulo in 1922, Mario de Andrade struck a match and then lit the fuse to several sticks of dynamite; the explosions so far have been much more than big noises. Earth has been moved, rock torn away, mines opened up for the digging of vast literary wealth. In fact, in this land famous for its aquamarine, amethyst, and royal topaz, many brilliant semi-precious stones sparkle under a tropic sun. Here and there, one catches sight of the deeper brilliance of ruby, sapphire, and diamond. So dazzling are some of the jewels in Brazil's literary case that it will take expert criticism quite a while to arrive at a just and proper appraisal. This anthology is intended, in a small way, to help facilitate such an appraisal.

São Paulo, Brazil   J. N.
December 1961

MANUEL BANDEIRA

(1 8 8 6 —)

Poetica

I am sick of limited lyricism
Of well-behaved lyricism
Of public-servant lyricism
With its time-clock card
And its clerkly protocol
And its ass-kissing flattery of the boss.

I am sick of halting lyricism
That has to look up in the dictionary
The vernacular meaning of a word.

Down with the purists!

I want all the words
Chiefly the universal barbarisms
I want all the constructions
Chiefly the syntactical ones of exception
I want all the rhythms
Chiefly the unnumbered.

I am sick of flirting lyricism
Of political lyricism
Of rickety lyricism
Of syphilitic lyricism

Of all lyricism which surrenders
To anything which is not its true self.

After all, that is not lyricism
That is only bookkeeping
A table of co-sines
A handbook for the perfect lover
With a hundred models of letters
And the different ways to please the ladies.

I prefer the lyricism of madmen
The lyricism of drunkards
The difficult and poignant lyricism of drunkards
The lyricism of Shakespeare's fools.

I will have nothing more to do
With a lyricism which is not freedom.

Pneumothorax

Fever, lung-coughing blood, gasping, and night-sweats.
A whole life that could have been, but was not.
Cough, cough, cough.

He sent for the doctor:
—Say thirty-three.
—Thirty-three . . . thirty-three . . . thirty-three . . .
—Breathe.

.   .   .   .

—You have a hole in the left lung and seepage into the right.
—Well, doctor, isn't it possible to try a pneumothorax?
—No. The only thing you can do is play an Argentine tango.

Moment in a Café

When the funeral procession passed by
The men who were in the café
Tipped their hats oh, so mechanically
In perfunctory and absent-minded salute to the dead
For they themselves were all turned toward life
They were swallowed up in life.
They were relying upon life.

One of them, however, swept off his hat
In the long and slow arc of a gesture
And stared at the hearse:
For this man knew that life is a fierce and aimless agitation
That life is a treason
And he paid his respects to the flesh which passed by
Forever freed from the dead soul.

Absolute Death

To die.
To die body and soul.
Completely.

To die without leaving the sad remains of flesh,
Without leaving the bloodless mask of wax,
Surrounded by flowers,
Which will rot away—so happy!—one day,
Bathed in tears
Born less from grief than from the shock of death.

To die without leaving perhaps even a pilgrim soul . . .
On the way to heaven?
But what heaven can fulfill your dream of heaven?

To die without leaving a furrow, a trace, a shadow,
Without leaving even the remembrance of a shadow
In any human heart, in any human thought,
In any human skin.

To die so completely
That one day when somebody sees your name on a page
He will ask: "Who was he? . . ."

To die still more completely:
Without leaving even this name.

Apple

From one angle I see you just like a dried-up breast
From another just like a belly from whose navel still hangs the
    umbilical cord

You are red as the divine love

Inside you in the little seeds
Palpitates a prodigious life
Infinitely

And you remain so simple
Beside a knife
In a poor hotel room.

Profundamente

When last night I fell asleep
At the feast of St. John
There was much merriment and noise
Stacatto banging of rockets and lights of Roman candles
Voices songs and laughter
Near the kindled bonfires.

In the middle of the night I awoke
And could no longer hear voices and laughter
Only vagrant balloons
Drifted here and there
Oh, so silently
And from time to time
Only the clatter of the streetcar
Bored through the silence
Like a tunnel.
Where were those who a mere moment ago
Were dancing
Were singing
Were laughing
Near the kindled bonfires?

—They were all asleep
They were all lying down
Sleeping
Oh, so profoundly.

When I was six years old
I could not see the end of the feast of St. John
Because I fell asleep.

Today I can no longer hear the voices of that time
My grandmother

My grandfather
Totonio Rodrigues
Tomasia
Rosa
Where are they all?

—They are all asleep
They are all lying down
Sleeping
Oh, so profoundly.

Roundel of the Little Horses

The little horses running,
And we, the big horses, eating . . .
And your beauty, Esmeralda,
Finally drove me mad.

The little horses running,
And we, the big horses, eating . . .
And the sun outside so bright,
But in my heart night is falling.

The little horses running,
And we, the big horses, eating . . .
Alfonso Reyes going away,
And so many people staying behind.

The little horses running,
And we, the big horses, eating . . .
Italy bragging and bullying,
And Europe coming apart at the seams . . .

The little horses running,
And we, the big horses, eating . . .
Brazil busy politicking,
My God! Poetry dying . . .
And the sun outside so bright,
And the sun so bright, Esmeralda,
But in my heart—night is falling!

I Am Going Away to Pasargada

I am going away to Pasargada
There I am friend of the king
There I have the woman I want
On the bed that I shall choose
I am going away to Pasargada.

I am going away to Pasargada
Here I am not happy
There life is an adventure
In such a non-mattering way
That Joan the Mad Woman of Spain
Queen and pretended insane
Is relative once removed
From the daughter-in-law I never had.

And how I will exercise!
I will pedal the bicycle!
I will ride the wild ass!
I will climb the greased pole!
I will bathe in the sea!
And when I am tired
I will lie on the banks of the river

And call the nymph of the water
To tell me the stories
That Rose used to tell me
When I was a boy
I am going away to Pasargada.

There's everything in Pasargada
It's another civilization:
It has a safe and sure way
To prevent knocking the girls up
It has automatic telephone
It has plenty of dope
It has beautiful prostitutes
For one to make love to.

And when I become sadder
So sad that I have no more hope
And when in the night it comes:
The desire to kill myself
—Ah, there I am friend of the king—
Then I have the woman I want
On the bed that I shall choose
I am going away to Pasargada.

Last Song of the Dead End

Dead End which I sang in a couplet
Full of mental ellipses,
Dead End of my sorrows,
Of my doubts and my fears
(But also of my loves,
Of my kisses, of my dreams),
Goodbye, goodbye forever!

They are going to tear down this house.
But my room will remain,
Not like an imperfect form
In this world of appearances:
It will remain in eternity,
With its books, with its pictures,
Intact, suspended in air!

Dead End of the evergreen thorn,
Of the passions with no tomorrows,
How much Mediterranean light
Did not the dew of the wee hours
Did not the purity of the mornings
Harvest upon these stones
With the shining of adolescence!

Dead End of my sorrows,
I am not ashamed of you!
Were you a street of the whores?
They are all daughters of God!
And before them there were the nuns . . .
And you belonged to the poor only
When, poor myself, I came to live here.

Lapa—Lapa do Desterro—,
Lapa which sins so much!
(But when six o'clock strikes,
In the first voice of the bells,
What angelic graces you have:
Like in that voice which announced
To Mary the conception of Christ!)

Our Lady of Carmel,
There from the height of the altar,

Is begging for alms for the poor—
For all the sad women,
For all the black women,
Who come at night to seek shelter
In the doorways of the church.

Dead End born in the shadows
Of the stone walls of convents,
You are life, life which is holy
No matter how many its falls.
For this I love you always,
And I sing to you to say:
Goodbye, goodbye forever!

The Morning Star

I want the morning star
Where is the morning star?
My friends my enemies
Hunt for the morning star

Naked she vanished
Vanished with whom?
Seek her everywhere

Call me a man without pride
A man who puts up with everything
What do I care?
I want the morning star

Three days and three nights
I was assassin and suicide
Thief, pimp, forger

O evil-sexed virgin
Tormentor of the afflicted
Two-headed giraffe
Sin for us all sin with us all

Sin with the hoods
Sin with the cops
Sin with the marines
Sin every way possible
With the Greeks and with the Trojans
With the priest and with the sexton
With the leper from the isolation ward

And then with me
I will wait for you with amusement parks carnivals rodeos
   I will eat earth and say things
   of such simple tenderness

That you will swoon

Hunt for her everywhere
Pure or degraded to the uttermost vileness
I want the morning star.

MARIO DE ANDRADE

(1 8 9 3 – 1 9 4 5)

MARIO DE ANDRADE

Impromptu of the Dead Boy

Dead, he rests sweetly among the flowers in his coffin.

There are such moments when we living
This life of interests and struggles
Grow tired of plucking desires and worries.
Then we stop a moment, leave the murmur of the body,
The lost head ceases to imagine,
And oblivion comes sweetly.
Who then can enjoy the roses around him?
The beautiful sight that the car cuts through?
The thought that makes him a hero? . . .
The body is a veil upon the furniture,
A gesture that stopped in the middle of the road,
A gesture we have forgotten.
Dead, he sweetly forgets among the flowers in his coffin.

He doesn't seem to sleep, nor do I say he dreams happily;
    he is dead.
In a moment of life the spirit forgot and stopped.
Suddenly he was frightened by the noise of tears,
Perhaps he felt a great frustration
For having left life while so strong and so young,

He felt spite and did not move any more.
And now he will not move any more.

Go away! go away, dead boy!
Oh, go away: I do not know you any more.
Do not return at night to flash on my destiny
The light of your presence and your desire to think!
Do not offer me again your courageous hope,
Nor ask of me the shape of the Earth for your dreams!

The universe bellows with grief at the flaming of fires,
The terrified alarms cross in the air,
And my peace is enormous and unbearable!
My tears fall upon you and you are like a broken Sun.
What freedom in your obilivion!
What firm independence in your death!
Oh, go away: I do not know you any more!

Aspiration

The sweetness of poverty like this . . .
To lose everything yours, even the egoism of being,
So poor that you can only belong to the crowd. . . .
I gave away everything mine, I spent all my being,
And I possess only what in me is common to all . . .
The sweetness of poverty like this. . . .

I am not lonely any more, I am dissolved among equal men!

I have walked. Along my way
The emphatic mark of my steps
Remained on ground wet with morning dew.

Then the Sun ascended, heat vibrated in the air
In golden particles of light and warm breath.

The ground burned and hardened.
The mark of my feet is now invisible . . .
But the Earth remains, the tenderly dumb Earth,
And growing, grieving, dying in Earth,
The always equal men remain. . . .

And I feel larger, equalizing myself to the equal men! . . .

Variation on the Bad Friend

At last, we are no longer friends.

You walk easily, lightly,
In the labyrinth of complications.
What subtlety! what dancing grace! . . .
It is true that there always remains
Some dust from your wings
On the branches, on the thorns,
Even on the blossoms of that wood . . .
And I also noticed several times
That your wings are ragged at the edges . . .
But the essential thing, the important thing,
Is that despite the raggedness you can still fly.

I am not like that.
I am heavy, I am rather clumsy,
I have no wings and not much breeding.
I need a broad and straight road.
If I lack space, I break everything,
I get hurt, I get tired . . . I finally fall.

In the middle of the wood I stop, unable to go on.
I cannot stand it any longer.

You . . . you may still call me a friend . . .
Although you lose a bit of your wing,
You sit on my thorn bush and can still fly.
Yet I, I suffer it is true,
But I am no longer your friend.
You are friend of the sea, you are friend of the river. . . .

The Mountains of Rolling-Girl

The Mountains of Rolling-Girl
Had not that name before . . .

They were from the other side,
They rode to town to marry.
And they crossed the mountains,
The bridegroom with his bride,
Each one on a horse.

Both of them were happy,
In the heavens all was peace.
Along the narrow trails
He rode ahead and she behind.
And they laughed. O how they laughed!
They laughed for no reason at all.

The Mountains of Rolling-Girl
Had not that name before.

The red tribes of evening

Rapidly rode away
And hurriedly hid themselves
Down down in the caves,
Afraid of the coming night.

But both of them continued,
Each one on a horse,
And they laughed. O how they laughed!

And their laughter married
With laughter of the pebbles
Which leaped so lightly
From the narrow path
Towards the precipice.

Ah, Fortune inviolate!
One hoof has stepped in error.
The bride and her horse vaulted
Headlong down the chasm.
Not even the thud was heard.
There is only the silence of death.
In the heavens all was peace . . .
Spurring and whipping his horse,
The bridegroom vaulted headlong
Into the void of the chasm.

And the Mountains of Rolling-Girl
Rolling-Girl were named.

Moment

The wind cuts everything in two.
Only a wish for neatness binds the world. . . .

There is sun. There was rain. And the wind
Scatters trombones of cloud in the blue.

Nobody can be whole in this city.
The doves cling to skyscrapers, it rains.
It is cold. It is heartache. . . . It is this violent wind
That bursts from the caves of human earth
Demanding sky, peace, and a touch of spring.

Streets of My São Paulo

Streets of my São Paulo:
Where is the living love,
Where is it?

Roads of the city:
I run after my friend,
Where is he?

Streets of my São Paulo:
Love greater than food,
Where is it?

Roads of the city:
An answer to my request,
Where is it?

Streets of my São Paulo:
The fault of the restless one,
Where is it?

It must be in the past:
In the damned centuries,
There it is.

That Man Who Walks All Alone

That man who walks all alone
Along those squares, those streets,
Has in himself an enormous secret.
    He is a man.

That woman like all the others
Along those squares, those streets,
Has in herself a cruel surprise.
    She is a woman.

The woman meets the man,
They smile and hold hands,
The surprise and the secret expand
    Violently.

But the shadow of the restless one
Guards that mystery in the dark.
Death watches with her scythe.
    Verily, it is night.

Song of the Corner

A little before noon
I felt she was coming. I waited.
She came. She passed. It was as though
The Moon had passed
Along this strange path
I have walked since birth.

The all-green belljar
Of my breast darkened.

Night of kindhearted May.
There goes the Moon passing by.
There is indeed a refraction
That winds round my neck
The scarf of the Milky Way
And the Moon over my hand.

But when I seek to enjoy
The beautiful touch of moonlight,
And I stroke with my hand my fingers . . .
I have to admit my delusion.
It was the lie of the senses,
It was the dew. Nothing more.
It came. It passed. It was as though
The Moon. . . .

I sigh and am a child again.
—What do you want, Mario?—Mother,
I want the Moon!—Impossible today,
She has already gone. Be patient,
I will give you the Moon tomorrow.

And I wait. You wait . . . He waits . . .

Oh, beans!

Moment

Somewhere near, a rose-tree must be blooming,
I don't know . . . I feel in myself a harmony,
Some of the disinterest that fatigue brings.

I look at my hands. And a dangerous tenderness
Makes me touch them with my lips, lightly.
(It must be some rose . . .)
Tenderness that is no longer dangerous, no, patient pity.
The roses . . . The millions of roses from São Paulo . . .
I have so often seen my hands work,
And strike in fun the back of a friend,
Give themselves to enemies, and pick up money
     from the ground . . .
Once my fingers rested on two lips,
And I wished I were blind at that moment!
She did not kiss my finger tips,
She kissed my hands, with passion, in submission . . .
She kissed the dust of my hands . . .
The same dust that drifts on the rose as it opens.
Somewhere near, a rose-tree must be blooming . . .
What harmony in me . . . How like a garden . . .
My body is healthy . . . My soul went away . . .
And left me.

Rondeau for You

to Couto de Barros (1924)

From you, Rose, I do not like
To accept only this slow hug
That you give me
Or only this moist kiss
That you give me . . .
I do not for a single reason:
From everything you tell me
I see that in your breast
Sobs the well-made heart
     of you.

And then I imagine
That together with the slender body
The dark little body
That you give me
Together with your loveliness
The maddening charm and laughter
That you give me
It would be something if I too owned
What hides behind your face, Rose:
The thought, the soul, the grief
     of you.

from Poems of the Woman Friend

I

The sun was setting in my eyes
And the flight of the hour surrendered me April,
A familiar taste of goodbye nourished
An air and, I don't know why, I saw you.

I turned me into a flower. But it was scarcely
   your memory.
You were away, sweet friend; and I saw only
   in the profile of the city
The strong archangel of a pink skyscraper
Beating his blue wings against the twilight.

II

Maybe if we had kissed one time only. . . .
Yesterday you were so beautiful
That my body drew near.
I know it was a brook and two hours of thirst,
I bent down, I did not drink.

But I have remained the same until now,
Watching four or five yellow butterflies,
Ordinary ones, frolicking in air.
I hear a sound. . . .

III

Now it is April, oh my sweet friend,
You leaned over me, like the truth,
I tried to turn and I fixed my face to your body.

We mastered ourselves and put everything in its place.
The sky resumed its position over the earth,
The orange trees all stood up
And in them we made the first sabiá sing.

But the landscape soon went away
Slamming the door, terribly scandalized.

The Girl and the Goat

The girl fights to pull the goat,
Totally terrified, sliding on the pavement
Among the bells of the streetcars
And the speed of the dusty automobiles.

. . . A whole herd of goats . . .
The goats graze on the mid-day grass . . .
And in the dead solitude of the mountain
Not a single sound of a car horn.
Ugly dog with big eyes hidden in his hair.
Near the stones moved by the little lizards,
Where the hot sun flounders in the troubled water,
Fixes his teeth in the golden cheese
Licias, the herdsman.

JORGE DE LIMA

(1893-1953)

The Words Will Resurrect

The words have grown old inside men
And separated into islands,
The words have mummified in the mouths of legislators;
The words have rotted in the promises of tryants;
The words mean nothing in the speeches of politicians.
And the Word of God is one despite the sacrilege
    of the men of Babel,
Despite the sacrilege of the men of today.
And can it be that the immortal word will sicken?
And can it be that the great Semitic word will disappear?
And can it be that the poet was not designated to give
    the word new life?
To pick it from the surface of the waters and offer it
    again to the men of the continent?
And was he not appointed to restore its essence,
    and to reconstitute its magic content?
Does the poet not see the communion of languages,
When men will reconquer the attributes lost with The Fall,
And when the nations founded after Babel will be destroyed?
When all the confusion is undone,
Will the poet not speak from wherever he is,

To all the men on earth, in one single language—
   the language of the Spirit?
But should you live sunk in time and in space,
You will not understand me, brother!

Distribution of Poetry

I took wild honey from the plants,
I took salt from the waters, I took light from the sky.
Listen, my brothers: I took poetry from everything
To offer it to the Lord.
I did not dig gold from the earth
Or leech blood from my brothers.
Inn-keepers: let me alone.
Peddlers and bankers:
I can fabricate distances
To keep you away from me.
Life is a failure,
I believe in the magic of God.
The roosters are not crowing,
The day has not dawned.
I saw the ships go and return.
I saw misery go and return.
I saw the fat man in the fire.
I saw zig-zags in the darkness.
Captain, where is the Congo?
Where is the Isle of Saint Brandon?
Captain, what a black night!
Mastiffs howl in the darkness.
O Untouchables, which is the country,
Which is the country that you desire?
I took wild honey from the plants.

I took salt from the waters, I took light from the sky.
I have only poetry to give you.
Sit down, my brothers.

Papa John

Papa John withered like a rootless stick.—
    Papa John is going to die.
Papa John rowed the boats.—
    He dug the earth.
    He made spring from the ground
    The emerald of leaves—coffee, cane, cotton.
Papa John dug up more emeralds
    Than pioneer Paes Leme.

Papa John's daughter had the breasts of a cow
    For his master's children to suck:
    When her breasts dried up, Papa John's daughter
    Also withered while fastened to
    A pressing iron.
    Papa John's skin stuck to the tips
    Of whips.
    Papa John's strength stayed on the handle
    Of hoe and of scythe.
    Papa John's wife the white
    Man stole and made her a nurse.
Papa John's blood dissolved in the good blood
    Like a lump of crude sugar
    In a pan of milk.—
    Papa John was a horse for his master's children to mount.
    Papa John could tell such beautiful stories
    That you felt like crying.

Papa John is going to die.
The night outside is as black as Papa John's skin.
Not one star in the sky.
It looks like the witchcraft of Papa John.

The River and the Serpent

The river and the serpent are mysterious, my son.
On the top of that mountain
Were two circles of the Eternal.
One circle was the serpent,
The other circle was the river:
Both precipitated,
Both came searching for man,
One to purify him,
The other to poison him.
Down there they both found
The simple man.
One offered him the Fish to feed him,
The other offered him the fruit to intoxicate him.
The river and the serpent are mysterious, my son.
From the clouds they precipitated,
Both are crawling on the earth
Like the two ways of man,
For him to choose as his guide.
The river and the serpent are mysterious, my son:
They come from the beginning of things,
They run towards the end of everything,
And sometimes in the water of the river
You will find the black serpent.
Things were simple, my son,
But they became confused:

The river that washes you
Can also drown you,
For under the appearance of the river
Slides the serpent.
The river and the serpent are mysterious, my son:
In the beginning they were two circles,
From there they came uncoiled.

The Multiplication of the Creature

It seems, Lord, that I have unfolded myself,
That I have multiplied myself,
That the rain from heaven falls into my hands,
That the noise of the world moans in my ears,
That someone husks wheat, weeping, on my naked trunk,
That cities burn within my eyesockets.
It seems, Lord, that the nights darken in my manifold being,
That I speak unwittingly for all my brothers,
That I walk more and more in search of You.
It seems, Lord, that You have lengthened my arms
To reach for rare and gleaming vaults,
That You have extended my feet resting in Limbo,
That the tired birds perch on my shoulder
Without knowing that the scarecrow is Your Image.
It seems that in my veins
Flow the nocturnal rivers
Where boatmen row against rising tides.
It seems that in my shadow
The sun rises and sets,
And my shadow and my being
Are worth one minute in You.

The Sleep Before

Stop everything that keeps me from sleep:
Those cranes in the night,
That violent wind,
The last thought of those suicides.
Stop everything that keeps me from sleep:
Those internal ghosts that open my eyelids,
This acceleration of my heart,
This echoing of things deserted and dumb.
Stop everything that keeps me from returning
    to the sunlit sleep
That God gave me
Before He created me.

I Announce Consolation to You

1—The poor who possess only their poverty
    And nothing else;
    The dying who count on their end only
    And nothing else;
    The weak who possess only their weakness
    And nothing else,
    Can walk on the waters of the sea.

2—Those who possess herds of machines,
    Those who are heavy with crimes and gold,
    Men of hatred or of pride;
    Those will sink.

3—We will call the man whom war has almost devoured
    And to whom it has left only his knees on the ground.
    That man will run faster than light.

4—We will call the man who blew out the life that
    God gave him,
  And whom the evil of the earth has spoiled with
    its vices.
  That man, God will give him new life.

5—We will call the man who saw the first minute. And
    he died.

6—The man who wanted to smile and was born without lips.

7—These will be comforted.
  These will remain at the right hand.

Rag Doll

Rag doll with eyes of bead,
a dress of chintz,
hair of ribbons,
stuffed with wool.

Day and night, her opened eyes,
looking at the toy soldiers that can march,
at the jacks-in-the-box that can jump.
Rag doll that falls down:
she does not break, she costs a penny.
Rag doll of the unhappy girls
who lead the cripples, who pick up
cigarette butts, who beg at the corners, poor things!
Rag doll with an impassive face like those girls.
Dirty little doll, stuffed with wool.—
The eyes of bead have fallen off. Blind

she rolls in the gutter. The garbage man takes her away,
covered with mud, naked,
Just as our Lord had intended.

Christmas Poem

O, my Jesùs, as soon as you grow
A little bit older,
Come take a walk with me,
For I too am fond of children.

We shall go see the tame beasts
In the zoological garden.
And on any holiday
We shall then go, for example,
To see Christ King of Corcovado.

And those who pass
Upon seeing the boy
Will certainly say: There goes the son
Of Our Lady of the Immaculate Conception!

—That little boy who goes there
(Several men will then add)
Knows more things than all of us.

—Good morning, Jesus—a voice will say.

And other voices will whisper:
—It is the handsome boy who is in the book
Of my First Communion.

—How strong he looks!—Nothing changed!
—How healthy he looks! What fine coloring!
(Other gentlemen will say a little later on).

But other people of different appearance
Will surely say on seeing You:
—It is the son of the carpenter!
And on seeing the custom of a working man
To take a walk on a Sunday,
They will invite us to go together
To visit our fellow workers.

And when we come back
Home, at night,
And the sinners turn to their vices,
They will undoubtedly ask me.

And I will invent subtle excuses
For You to let me go alone.
Child Jesus, have mercy on us,
Hold my hand very tight.

Goodbye to Poetry

My Lord Jesus, this century is rotten.
Where shall I seek for poetry?
I must take off all the cloaks,
The beautiful cloaks that the world has given me.
I must take off the cloak of poetry.
I must take off the purest cloak.
My Lord Jesus, this century is sick,
This century is rich, this century is fat.

I must take off what is beautiful, I must take off poetry,
I must take off the purest cloak
Which time has given me, which life gives me.
I want Your road to be light.
Even what is beautiful is heavy on my shoulders,
Even poetry above the world,
Above time, above life,
Mashes me on the earth, binds me to things.
I want a voice stronger than the poem,
Stronger than hell, stronger than death:
I want a power closer to You.
I want to strip myself of my voice and my eyes,
Of the other senses, of the other prisons;
I cannot, Lord: the age is sick.
The cries of the earth, of suffering men
Bind me, pull me—give me Your hand.

CASSIANO RICARDO

(1 8 9 5 —)

M'Orpheus

I

Dream, the only god who inhabits
our house—the unique memory
that we have had wings—
and who still corrects
—while we are apparently dead—
what there is of malediction in our body.

Under the anesthesia of sleep, while
we are horizontal,
as on a nocturnal
operation table.
He shapes, with the chisel of a feather, the statue
that is sleeping.

So that we can still see, not only
life, which is the real thing
(the night is a cemetery of words)
but also something beyond us,
and in spite of us.

II

And because dream is the image of poetry
and sleep is the brotherly being of death,

Orpheus is separated from Morpheus only
by a secret M.
By an M that only the dead man knows
after he has understood nothing.
(Because it is labial, and grave.)

The Four Angels

They are not more than four.
But they surround me, and inform me
of the harshest truth to be heard.
And they make me bow my head.

Ah, the angels who jump over the wall,
who smoke behind God's back, who utter
obscene things, those are not
the ones who disappoint me; the angel who wept three times
before speaking, that is the one.

The angel of shining feet, who will blow again the trumpet
of Jericho, that is not the one.

These are the four angels who, perhaps accidentally,
made me cry.
And who play around me, while I weep blood,
and while the snow falls.

Just now these four angels have told me
a terrible word.

Tantalus

What wayfarer
traced lines on the sand

of my desert?
What tragic drouth
is that which dehydrates
the blue windowpane
wherein I was
the witness?

What ache of sand
dries out my soul,
shrivels my fingernail?
From lack of water
the clepsydra dies.
An awful gravel
glasses my eyes.

Ah, if I cannot
shed my tears,
I have bayed the moon.
Stupid tears
that do not satisfy me.
How can I dry
my face
if I wept
as though I did not weep?
if the moon is a wailing
that cannot be wiped?

If the white disc
has limned silver
on my map of the world
and sewn screams
onto my flight?

I have bayed the moon.
But does it avail
my having wept for her

if the dry wailing
hurts me deeper
because it is bottomless
if it is useless
to encompass the world
and still remain
in this prison of glass?

If the great tears
of aquamarine
do not please me
because they are not mine?

It would be better for me
to be a simple fish
in the waves of the sea.
Only to have eyes
but not for weeping . . . .

The Hidden Rose

Against the demon of lucidity the birds sing.

What I seek is not in any photograph.

It is before me, hidden from myself and the Night.

The river from which I have drunk my tears is not
    on any map.

I must be on the earth for the contemplation of stars.

Ah, misfortunate
he who lives on the earth without seeing the stars,

he who has feet to lead his body,
full of deaf and absurd demands,
but has no hands to go pluck a rose.

The Other Life

I do not hope for another life, after this one.
If this one is bad
why should it not please the gods,
the pain I have already suffered?
If life is good, it will cease to be good
if repeated.

Masochism

I
O mad wind, lash
me.
I want to be the daring bird
whose feathers you pluck
in the wild bush.

O Turkish moon, kill
me,
without any shame,
drilling my eyes
with your silver horns.

O blind wave, take
me,
in your fierce emerald,

as a drunkard is taken,
into the green darkness.

II

And the ant, which cuts
its own proper wings,
like one who contradicts himself,
stripping itself, nimbly,
of that which made it
happy?

And this need,
with which at times I inflame myself,
of getting rid
of those things which I love best?

Zoo

Here they are: the pink hippopotami.
Here are the futuristic rhinoceri, the zebras
which the hand of God has striped black and silver
to give us proofs of an exact geometry.

The graceful giraffes, with such long necks
that can reach the blooms of a palm tree,
if a palm tree should blossom, and the coarse elephants
whose trunks sport with objects in the air.

In spite of their cubic bodies and rhomboid feet.
(So tame that on their backs pigeons coo,
so dense that night lives in their eyes.)
And the white bears, that have contemplated,

happier than we, a polar star.
Some give the impression of a ferocity
fully pervasive and, therefore, tranquil; others demand
of the onlookers a deeper thought about origin,

of where they came from to this arrival—the black mystery
of which they are the long-ago and far-away bearers.
Others so ornamental that they look rather like
immense lilies for a class

in botany, or else in geography,
or of anything human that may exist in a cage.
I think of the animals which Noah took
into his ark, in that wild and Biblical time,

when men and animals were flowers, or,
at least, they lived together in one and the same
comradeship—Biblical time that has passed
but—who knows? (I think) has not yet died.

I think of the scene of Daniel among the lions,
of Saint Francis, who called the wolf his brother.
And I ask again: why doesn't man,
who today is made more of wing than of belly,

come and contemplate them, like the children
for whom all the beasts are toys
and all the serpents colorful and tame?
(For me, nothing more logical than a zoo

whose only sadness is that of the flightless birds.)
Why doesn't he come and contemplate them, before
the geometric bird drops a star upon the earth?
(Because the children who today peer through the grates

at the russet beasts are already orphans of this war.)
Why doesn't he come and contemplate them (if not for this)
at least in order to compare his own ferocity
with that of those beasts today so serene,

under the mysterious joy of those colors
with which they adorn the world—the world now deaf
and absurd—where a zoological garden
is like an island, a golden marvel

where wild animals are flowers—pathetic flowers
that the uranium sun will make innocent.
For what is today a zoological garden, finally,
what is it but a lesson of universal love?

The Banquet

In my bedroom, silence
and a lamp that cuts me in two.
My bedroom is poorer than Job's:
two of me and one single lamp.

In the drawing room of my neighbor,
who has not invited me, the white table;
and the guests drinking a sad wine.
Could that be the blood of Orpheus? Lachryma-Christi?

But if the wine is sad,
there are liquid stars in tall glasses
that shine, like geometric lilies,
lifted in air at the hour of delirium.

I feel good, thus,
uninvited, because I do not drink stars
or blood; I am a stepson of joy.
Sadness is my daily bread.

At the party I would be
an insult to the others, something comic.
A stone for those who have wings on their shoulders.
A lump of coal when everything there is aflame.

I feel good, because
I am a cactus with leaves of silence.
I would not trade my nocturnal and submarine
being for any swallow of wine.

Therefore let me hear only
the tinkle of the glasses, the confused
trilling of the Bacchantes. It only pleases me
to drink—rose in a tumbler—the dawn.

Ah, if they all knew
the good they have done me by exclusion
from the banquet—the most logical of oversights—
they would extend a toast to the uninvited.

Pastoral Ode

The landscape is mine
merely because I have eyes.
The bird is mine
only because I have ears.

I love with my hand the things
which my being here has given me.
In the universal green,
I am my being, I am not myself.

In my lyrical lexicon
exist only two words,
and one is sister to the other:
the morning and the morrow.

I feel that space is life
and that time is death.
And I place between one and the other
my flock of stars.

CECILIA MEIRELES

(1 9 0 1 —)

CECILIA MEIRELES

Introduction

Here is my life:
This sand so clear
With drawings that walk
Dedicated to the wind . . .

Here is my voice:
This empty shell
The shadow of a sound
Preserving its own lament . . .

Here is my grief:
This broken coral
Surviving its pathetic moment . . .

Here is my heritage:
This solitary sea—
On one side it was love
And on the other forgetfulness.

Portrait

I did not have this face of today
So calm

So sad
So thin.

Nor these eyes so empty
Nor this bitter mouth.

I did not have these strengthless hands
So still
And cold
And dead.

I did not have this heart
That does not even show itself.

I did not realize this change
So simple
So certain
So easy.

In what mirror did I lose my face?

Motive

I sing because the moment exists
And my life is complete.
I am not gay, I am not sad:
I am a poet.

Brother of fugitive things,
I feel no delight or torment.
I cross nights and days
In the wind.

Whether I destroy or build,
Whether I persist or disperse,
—I don't know, I don't know.
I don't know if I stay or go.

I know that I sing.
The song is everything.
The rhythmic wing has eternal blood,
And I know that one day I shall be dumb:
—Nothing more.

Guitar

Silver dagger you were,
Silver dagger!
It was not you who made
Such a fool of my hand.

I saw you shining among stones,
Silver dagger!
On your handle, blooming flowers,
On your blade, the exact measure,

The exact, the precise measure,
Silver dagger,
To cut through to my heart
With an initial and a date.

The greatest pain I have,
Silver dagger,
Is not to see me dying,
But to know who is killing me.

The Roosters Will Crow

The roosters will crow when we die,
And a soft breeze, with delicate hands,
Will touch the fringes, the silken
Shrouds.

And the sleep of night will cloud
The clear windows.

And the crickets, far off, will saw silences:
Stalks of crystal, cold long solitudes,
And the enormous perfume of trees.

Ah, what sweet moon will look upon our calm face,
Even yet more calm than her great mirror
Of silver.

What thick freshness upon our hair,
As free as the fields at sunrise.

From the mist of dawn,
One last star
Will ascend: pale.

What immense peace, without human voice,
Without the lip of wolfish faces,
Without hatred, without love, without anything!

Like dark lost prophets,
Only the dogs will talk through the valleys.
Strong questions. Vast pauses.

We shall lie in death
In that soft contour
Of a shell in the water.

Medieval Sandal

Just a medieval
sandal.

O what is left of the dances,
of the tournaments and songs,
of the hopes,
of the lady friends and enemies
from a vague feudal time.

So small for the weight
of any shod life,
though now it is nothing,
what was it: love? contempt?
it has become supernatural.

Under the hem of whose dresses?
On what hard floors?
—Oh, heavy castles!—
What wounded hearts?
Among whose thoughts,
sad? innocent? beautiful?
treading upon Good and Evil . . .

In the brief world time,
the slender foot of a slender woman
has left this sandal
as a little token.

It is only a half step
in space.

Does the other lie in some deep entrance?

One half of the measure
of what final music?

Just a medieval
sandal.

Pastoral

Here is the tiny shepherd,
much smaller than his flock,
watching, timid and careful,
the sunset in the field,
hugging the little lamb
like a brother his own size.

His eyes are, in the silence,
more than a shepherd's—a saint's.

The blue and green horizon
is turning violet and red,
and all the clouds disappear,
and a star comes on
—to take away that boy
who is leading his flock.

Museum

Since the lords are already dead
and cannot fight any more,

their armored plates, with regret,
have sat them down to the game.

On the chessboard there the horses,
the towers, the soldiers, the king . . . A hand
of iron can almost reach to play;
it lacks only the articulation.

O briefly squared plain
of the chessboard!
Visors lonesome for blood,
for wars which time has undone.

O unsatisfied ghosts
of the lords who are no more!
How much of death, without wars,
you, beyond all wars, now engage!

The Archangel

The voice of the Archangel falls.

(From the top of colored towers,
among arrows and stained windows;
from the top of minarets; from the top
of Gothic steeples; from the height
of curved domes; from the fine
Golden Crescent; from the large
baroque belfries; from these
cold jesuitical triangles;
from the arms of the crosses; from the clouds,
from the trees, from the jet of water,

from the doves' wings, from the little
corolla of the frail anemone . . .)

The voice of the invisible Archangel falls.
Lonesome.
Solitary.

(Tell me if you have ever heard it,
thus: far off, full of sorrow, centuries old.)

The Gates of Midnight

The angels come to open the gates of midnight,
at that very moment when sleep is deepest
and silence most pervasive.

The gates wheel open and unexpectedly we sigh.

The angels come with their golden music,
their tunics billowing with celestial breezes,
and they sing in their fluid incomprehensible tongue.

Then the trees burst forth with blossoms and fruit,
the moon and the sun intertwine their beams,
the rainbow unwinds its ribbons
and all the animals appear,
mingled with the stars.

The angels come to open the gates of midnight.

And we understand that there is no more time,
that this is the last vision,

that our hands are already lifted for goodbyes,
that our feet at last are freed from the earth,
freed for that flight, announced and dreamed
since the beginning of births.

The angels extend us their divine invitations.
And we dream that we are no longer dreaming.

CARLOS DRUMMOND DE ANDRADE

(1 9 0 2 —)

Pathetic Poem

What kind of noise is that on the stairs?
It is love coming to an end,
It is the man who closed the door
And hanged himself in the curtains.

What kind of noise is that on the stairs?
It is Guiomar who covered her eyes
And blew her nose fortissimo.
It is the still moon upon the plates
And the cutlery shining in the pantry.

What kind of noise is that on the stairs?
It is the dripping of the water faucet,
It is the inaudible lament
Of someone who has lost his gamble
While the music of the band
Goes down, down, down.

What kind of noise is that on the stairs?
It is the virgin with a trombone,
The child with a drum,
The bishop with a bell,
And someone who pianissimos the noise
Which jumps from my heart.

Secret

You cannot communicate poetry.
Keep still in your corner.
Do not love.

I hear that there is shooting
Within reach of our body.
Is it a revolution? is it love?
Say nothing.

Everything is possible, only I am impossible.
The sea overflows with fish.
There are men who walk on the sea
As though they walked in the street.
Do not tell.

Suppose that an angel of fire
Swept the face of the earth
And the sacrificed men
Asked for mercy.
Beg nothing.

The Dirty Hand

My hand is dirty.
I must cut it off.
Useless to wash it.
The water is rotten.
Or to soap it.
The soap is no good.

The hand has been dirty
For many many years.

At first hidden
In the pocket of my trousers,
Who would know it?
People used to call me,
Offering me their hand.
Hard, I refused.
The hidden hand
Would spread its dark
Track through my body.
And I saw it was the same
To use it or put it away.
The disgust was the same.

Ah, how many nights
Way back in my house
I washed this hand,
I scrubbed it, I scoured it!
For greater contrast,
I wished I could turn it
Into crystal or diamond,
Or even, at last,
Into a simple white hand,
The clean hand of a man,
Which you could hold
And lift to your lips
Or clasp in your own
In one of those moments
When two people confess
Without saying a word . . . .
The incurable hand
Opened its dirty fingers.

It was a filthy dirt,
Not dirt of earth,
Not dirt of coal,
Not dirt of a scab,
Not sweat of a shirt
Of one who has worked.
It was a sad dirt
Made from disease
And from mortal anguish
In the disgusted skin.
It was not black dirt—
The black so pure
In a white thing.
It was gray-brown dirt,
Gray-brown, dull, thistle.

Useless to keep
The ignoble dirty hand
Lying upon the table.
Quick, cut it off,
And throw it into the sea!
With time, with hope
And its machinery,
Another hand will come,
Pure—transparent—,
And fasten itself to my arm.

Sadness in Heaven

In heaven also there is a melancholy hour.
A difficult hour, when doubt invades the souls.
Why did I make the world? God wonders
And answers: I do not know.

The angels look at Him in disapproval.
Their feathers fall.

All the hypotheses: grace, eternity, love
Fall. They are feathers.

One feather more, and heaven is undone.
So quiet, no breaking noise tells
The moment between everything and nothing.
That is to say, the sadness of God.

The Dead in Frock Coats

In a corner of the drawing room was an album
     of unbearable photographs,
Many meters high and infinite minutes old,
Over which everyone leaned
To make fun and to laugh at the dead in frock coats.

A worm began to eat the indifferent frock coats,
And he ate the pages, the dedications, and even
     the dust on the pictures.

The only thing he did not eat was the immortal
     sob of life
Which broke from those pages.

The Ox

O solitude of the ox in the field,
O solitude of man in the street!
Amid cars, trains, telephones,
Amid screams, the profound aloneness.

O solitude of the ox in the field,
O millions suffering without a curse!
Whether it is night or day makes no difference,
Darkness breaks up with the dawn.

O solitude of the ox in the field,
Men writhing without a word!
The city cannot be explained
And the houses have no meaning.

O solitude of the ox in the field!
The ghost ship passes
Silently through the crowded street.
If a love storm should blow up!
The hands clasped, the life saved . . .
But the weather is steady. The ox is alone.
In the immense field: the oil derrick.

Consolation at the Beach

Come on, don't cry . . .
Childhood is lost.
Youth is lost.
But life is not lost.

The first love is over.
The second love is over.
The third love is over.
But the heart goes on.

You have lost your best friend.
You haven't tried any traveling.

You own no house, ship, or land.
But you look at the sea.

You haven't written the perfect book.
You haven't read the best books
Nor have you loved music enough.
But you own a dog.

A few harsh words,
In a low voice, have hurt you.
Never, never have they healed.
But what about humor?

There is no resolution for injustice.
In the shadow of this wrong world
You have whispered a timid protest.
But others will come.

All summed up, you should
Throw yourself—once and for all—into the waters.
You are naked on the sand, in the wind . . . .
Sleep, my son.

Search for Poetry

Do not make verses about happenings.
For poetry, there is no creation or death.
In her eyes, life is an unmoving sun,
Which neither warms nor lights.
The attractions, the anniversaries, the personal incidents
    do not matter.

Do not make poetry with the body,
This excellent, complete and comfortable body, so unfit
    for lyrical flow.
Your drop of gall, your face-making of pleasure or of pain
    in the dark
Are of no account.
Do not tell me your feelings,
Which capitalize on ambiguity and attempt the long journey.
What you think and feel, that is not yet poetry.

Do not sing your city, leave it alone.
The song is not the movement of the machines or the secret
    of the houses.
It is not music heard in passing; nor the sound of the sea
    in the streets near the edge of spume.
The song is not nature
Or men in society.
For it, rain and night, fatigue and hope mean nothing.
Poetry (do not make poetry out of things)
Eliminates subject and object.

Do not dramatize, do not invoke,
Do not investigate. Do not waste time telling lies.
Do not be anxious.
Your ivory yacht, your diamond shoe,
Your mazurkas and superstitions, your family skeletons
Disappear in the curve of time, they are worthless.

Do not resurrect
Your buried and melancholy childhood.
Do not oscillate between the mirror
And your fading memory.
If it faded, it was not poetry.

If it broke, it was not crystal.

Penetrate deftly the kingdom of words:
Here lie the poems that wait to be written.
They are paralyzed, but not in despair,
All is calm and freshness on the untouched surface.
Here they are alone and dumb, in the state of the dictionary.
Before you write them, live with your poems.
If they are obscure, be patient. If they provoke you,
    hold your temper.
Wait for each one to actualize and to consume itself
In the power of language
And the power of silence.
Do not force the poem to come out of Limbo.
Do not pick from the ground the poem that was lost.
Do not flatter the poem. Accept it
As it will accept its own form, final and concentrated
In space.

Come closer and contemplate the words.
Each one
Has a thousand secret faces under a neutral face
And asks you, without interest in the answer,
Poor or terrible, which you will give it:
Have you brought the key?

Please note:
Barren of melody and meaning,
The words have taken refuge in the night.
Still humid and saturated with sleep,
They roll in a difficult river and turn themselves
    into despising.

Dawn

The poet was drunk in a streetcar.
Day was dawning behind the backyards.
The gay boarding houses were sleeping most sadly.
The houses also were drunk.

Everything was beyond repair.
Nobody knew the world was going to end
(Only a child guessed it but kept silent),
That the world was going to end at 7:45.
Last thoughts! final telegrams!
Joseph, who had mastered his pronouns,
Helen, who loved men,
Sebastian, who was bankrupting himself,
Arthur, who said nothing,
Set sail for eternity.

The poet is drunk, but
He listens to an invitation in the dawn:
Shall we all go dancing
Between the streetcar and the tree?

Between the streetcar and the tree
Dance, my brothers!
Although there is no music
Dance, my brothers!

Children are being born
With such spontaneity.
How marvelous is love
(Love and other products).
Dance, my brothers!
Death will come later,
Like a sacrament.

Aspiration

I do not want any longer the maternal adoration
Which finally exhausts us and then flashes in panic,
Neither do I want the feeling of a precious find
Like that of Katherine Kippenburg at the feet of Rilke.

And I do not want the love, under silly disguises,
Of that same nymph desolate in her hermitage,
Nor the constant search of thirst rather than of lymph,
And neither do I want the simple rose of sex,

Hidden, meaningless, in the hostels of the wind,
Just as I do not want the geometric friendship
Of souls who elected one another in a proud cultivation,
An overlapping, perhaps? of melancholy needs.

I aspire rather to a faithful indifference
But poised enough to sustain life
And, in its indiscrimination of cruelty and diamond,
Able to suggest the end without the injustice of prizes.

MURILO MENDES

(1 9 0 2 —)

MURILO MONTEIRO MENDES

USSR

USSR
USSR USSR
Foolish virgin
Why don't you buy oil for your lamp?
Why do you think only of immediate and finite things?
USSR USSR
One day the Bridegroom will come,
He will give a great cry and it will be late.
You were dealing with your tractors,
You were busy only with the production of your
    collective farms,
And you did not notice that the Bridegroom was coming:
He shut Himself up in the red room with your sisters.
USSR

USSR USSR
Sweep your houses, your parks, of culture.
Send up in space your planes, light your reflectors,
Call your neighbors because you have found the lost ruble,
The Eternal Word that nourished you without your
    knowing it.
USSR USSR

USSR
You have already scattered your goods
To seek what has existed in you since the beginning.
Return to your Father's house, where there are many mansions.
Return to the communion of the sons of God,
O prodigal, O generous.

You will hear the great symphony of the organs, of the bells,
Mixed with the whistles of the sirens of ships and
   of factories,
O sister gone astray.
USSR USSR USSR

Final Judgment of the Eyes

Your eyes will be judged
With much less clemency
Than the rest of your body.
Your eyes have lingered too much
On breasts and hips,
They have lingered too little
On the other eyes that exist
Here in this world of God.
They have lingered nearly nothing
On the hands of the poor
And on the bodies of the sick.
Your eyes will suffer
More than the rest of your body:
They will not be allowed to look upon
The purest creatures
Who are to be seen in the other world.

Look, Timeless

Who am I anyway?
I am the portrait of an ancestor.
I am that nightgown I wore
Many years ago.
I am the almost faded companion
Of a girl who necked with me
Many years ago.
I am a slow waltz
Itching in my ears.
I am a corpse, a grimace
That a few guys take, laughing,
Without flowers in a car.
I am a reprobate waiting for the final sentence!

Half Bird

The woman from the world's end
Gives food to the rose trees,
Gives water to the statues,
Gives dreams to the poets.

The woman from the world's end
Calls the light with a whistle,
Turns the virgin into stone,
Cures the tempest,
Changes the course of dreams,
Writes letters to the rivers,
Pulls me from eternal sleep
To her singing arms.

The Culprit

Not only will I blame
My parents and grandparents:
I will also sue the initial egg.
Everything is at fault.
Oh, primal nebular stuff:
Giddiness of smells
Of matters movements
Of lights and endless waves.
Wrap me up in the end of the world.
Tumble creation down:
We will go in a vertigo
Without beginning middle or end.

The Three Circles

I do not find consolation in churches.
You, monk, cannot tell me what Christ will say.
You have gathered the least part of Him . . .
And His body and His blood
Do not make life circulate through my body and blood.
You, woman, a limited creature like me,
You receive the best part of my cult.
(I am aware of my error!)
I love you for your elegance, for your lie,
    for your theatrical life.
And I cannot even rest my head on the stone of your body. . . .
Only you, Satan, never fail me for a single moment!

Spiritual Poem

I feel I am a fragment of God
As I am a remnant of a root,
A little of the water of the seas,
The stray arm of a constellation.

Matter thinks by command of God.
Matter is transformed and evolves by command of God.
Matter is varied and beautiful.
Matter is one of the visible forms of the Invisible.
Christ is the most handsome of the sons of man.
Churches are full of legs, breasts, hair
Everywhere, even on the altar itself.
There are great forces of matter on earth and in air
That intertwine, mate, and reproduce every moment
One thousand editions of the divine thoughts.
Matter is great and formidable:
Without it there is no poetry.

Poem Seen from the Outside

The Spirit of Poetry transports me
To the shapeless region where I spend long hours, motionless
In the silence before the Creation of things, terrifying.
Suddenly I extend my right arm into space and everything
    incarnates.

The fresh dung of voluptuousness warms the earth.
The fish germinate in the vastness of ocean.
The crowds rush to the public square.

Brothels and churches, lying-in hospitals and cemeteries
Stand up in air for Good and for Evil.

The diverse characters that I have encompassed
Separate from one another and found a community
Where I preside, now sad, now gay.

I am not God because I depart for Him.
I am a god because they depart for me.
We are all gods because we depart for one single end.

Destruction

I will die detesting the evil I have done
And without the force to do good.
I love the guilty as well as the innocent.
O Magdalen, you who have triumphed over the power of flesh,
You are closer to us than the Virgin Mary,
Exempt, ever since eternity, from the original sin.
O my brothers, we are more united by sin than by Grace!
We belong to the great community of despair
Which will last till the end of all ages.

Anonymity

A woman on the verandah
Leans over the sea
Contemplates the twin sea gulls
Expects a love letter.

The aerial cemetery shines
The clouds play a boxing game.

Girls pass by singing.

They do not know I am a poet
Or the love that is in me.

Two-edged Sword

The opposite always arrives:
Everything that one has not asked for.

The invisible insists:
Nobody sees his own handkerchief.

In the deserted plain
Our ghost cries
For his life that is ruining itself.

Blue ball, it has been blown
By the evil winds.

Pure spirit.
Ripe hell.

Gambling

Heads or tails?
God or the devil?

Love or desertion?
Activity or solitude?

The hand opens: tails.
God and the devil.
Love and desertion.
Activity and solitude.

Newest Prometheus

I wanted to kindle the spirit of life,
I wanted to recast my own mold,
I wanted to know the truth of things, of the elements;
I rebelled against God,
Against the pope, the bankers, the ancient school,
Against my family, against my love,
Then against work,
Then against laziness,
Then against myself,
Against my three dimensions:

Then the dictator of the world
Had me imprisoned on Sugar Loaf;
Come, squads of planes,
Beak away my poor liver—
I vomit gallons of gall,
I contemplate down there the daughters of the sea
Dressed in bathing suits, singing sambas,
I see the dawns, the evenings break
—Purity and simplicity of life!—
But I cannot ask for forgiveness.

AUGUSTO FREDERICO SCHMIDT

(1 9 0 6 —)

I Have Seen the Sea

I have seen the sea! Not this, but another!
I have seen the sea—a sea dark and without redemption.
I have seen the sea! The waves like useless words
Rising!

I have seen the sea!
It was an immense sea without skies.
A naked sea, with huge arms!
A sea of despair, now running,
Now motionless, in the silence of an open grave!

I have seen the sea, the great sea!
My eyes have journeyed over the moving masses!
I have seen the sea!
Oh! it was terrible as an unforgiving love!
I have seen the sea!
It had a vast likeness unto death.
It looked like the bed where death rests in her nights.

I have seen the sea!
It was the revelation of Death.
My heart was suspended.
My eyes wept!
I have seen the sea without heaven!

Not to Die

Not to die—but to be picked by death.
To be picked, because ripe, for silence.
Not to die—but to bend toward death,
Like the fruit which, touched by time,
Bows toward the moist earth.

Not to die—but to be with death ample and serene
In the eyes, in the heart and the body and the soul.
To be for the End, ripe as mulberries in season,
Like the mountain mulberries.

To feel in yourself the harmony of the ultimate pace
And the consolation of looks that do not want to see
    any more.
To be taken by the hand of death,
And to be with death in yourself, like hope, like
    the only hope.

Birth of Sleep

From the depth of the sky sleep will come.
Sleep will come growing through space,
Sleep will come walking through the earth,
And it will steal unawares upon the tired birds
And the flowers, the fish, and the old men.

Sleep will come from the sky and will glide,
Thickening, in the abandoned valleys.
Sleep will come soft and terrible,
And its hands will freeze the water of the rivers

And the petals of roses.
Its hands will undress the trees
And the bodies of children.

From the depth of the sky sleep will come;
And the throat of every man will cry silently,
And everything will fall asleep,
Head turned toward the abyss.

Preparation for Oblivion

The rain falls on the nevermore,
And it falls on the rare roses in the garden.
With the rain exaltation has turned into sadness,
And that which was destruction, lying and deception,
Is at this moment, for memory, only a dead child.

One Day I Will Meet You

One day I will meet you.
My secret will open like the evening flowers.
The distance of everything will descend upon your spirit.
And what today is incredible will be as simple as
    the growth of roots in the earth.

I will open my heart, and you will find yourself in it.
I will open my spirit to your lucid look,
And you will be surprised to find yourself there,
    you will be yourself,
—You, who are free from limitations,
You who approach mysteriously in the night,
You, you who are the impossible one.

Poem

The voice of poets lost in the unknown;
The sadness of those who have always been mistreated
And lived meekly without complaint;
The lonesomeness of the resigned, for whom
Life was a long exile;
The innocence insulted by the world,
In her quiet and frozen indifference:
—All this is set in your look,
All this is fixed in your face
Shining with the martyrdom of love,
All this is set in your countenance,
O star, O flower, O water pure and clear!
In your look full of shadow, in your veiled look,
Are imprisoned the tears that will quench my thirst
    in the acidic hour when the desert will be
    the end of my destiny!

Search for Christmas

I will walk in search of the manger
The whole night, my Lord.
But there won't be any star
To guide my steps:
All the stars will be motionless
In a motionless sky.

I will walk in search of the manger
The whole night, my Lord.
But the roads will be lonely.

Everything will be asleep,
The lights in the houses turned off,
The voices of pilgrims dead in the endless distance.

I will walk anxious, in search of You.
But I will be so late,
Time will have walked so far ahead of me,
That it will be very hard for me to find your humble
   corner—
Tired, I shall find enormous cities,
But Your City, Lord, will have disappeared.

Knowing that I seek You, many will laugh at me.

No star will shine
To show me where You are.
All the stars will remain motionless in heaven.

Destiny

Where are those who smiled
And were like new-born roses?
Where are those who were white and pure
As the waters that flow from high rocks
In the dense heart of the forest?

Where are those who were beautiful,
Those who had in their eyes the gleam of the stars?
Where are those who sang and wore bells and flowers
In the voice of dawn?

Where are those who danced as lightly
As flowers that the wind shakes and dispetals?
Where are those who carried in their jars
The water from living springs?

Where are those who filled the dark world
With the graceful smile of happiness?
Where are those who twined in their long black hair
The little red heart of a flower?

They are, my Lord, hidden—far away,
Where grow the roots of Your big trees.
They are hidden away, dispetaled in the moist night.

Genesis of Miracle

We are present at the process of miracles.
The drowned roses sinking in the chill of night.
Who will say the words that are going to deliver
    your heart from death?
The arms of the Cross accept the nocturnal winds
And the enormous tears and the great sobs.
Liberation rests in silence!
When the beggars fall asleep, poetry ascends
    to the pale skies.
Who will see the just man playing with the hair
    of the dead
And the lights advancing mercifully through darkness?

Someone inside the sea is crying.
The waters are smiling, mysterious and still.

Someone Is Sleeping in the Road . . .

Someone is sleeping in the road.
I don't know who he is.
I can only guess that he is a creature without worries
—Free from death and the feelings of doubt and despair.
I know that he is a creature exempt from ambitions
    and desires.
His sleep is as serene as the twilight strolling through
    the wheat fields.
His sleep is as simple as the unknown springs.
I don't see his face.
But he must have a long nose,
And the wrinkled forehead of a patriarch.
The wind, a fresh wind, full of the scent of the flowers
    in the field,
Caresses his white beard.

VINICIUS DE MORAIS
(1 9 1 3 —)

Imitation of Rilke

Someone who is watching me from the depth of night
With motionless eyes shining in the night
Wants me.

Someone who is watching me from the depth of night
(A woman who loves me, lost in the night?)
Calls me.

Someone who is watching me from the depth of night
(Is it you, Poetry, holding a vigil in the night?)
Wants me.

Someone who is watching me from the depth of night
(Death also comes from the solitudes of night ...)
Who is it?

Longing for Manuel Bandeira

You were not merely a secret
Of poetry and of emotion:
You were a star in my exile—
Poet, father! stern brother.

You not only took me to your bosom,
But you also gave me your hand:

117

I, very small—you, elect
Poet! father, stern brother.

Clear, tall and ascetic friend
Of the sad and pure heart:
What do you dream so much all by yourself—
Poet, father, stern brother?

The Acrobats

Let us go up!
Go up higher
Go up beyond, go up
Above beyond, let us go up!
With the physical possession of our arms
We will inexorably climb
The great oceans of stars
Through thousands of years of light.

Let us go up!
Like two acrobats
Our faces petrified
In the faint smile of effort
Let us go up farther
With the physical possession of our arms
And the measureless muscles
In the convulsive calm of ascension.

Oh, higher
Farther than everything
Beyond, farther than above beyond!
Like two acrobats
Let us go up, very slowly

There where infinity
Is so infinite
That it has not even a name
Let us go up!

Tense
By the luminous rope
Which hangs invisible
And whose knots are stars
Burning our hands
Let us rise to the surface
Of the huge ocean of stars
Where night sleeps
Let us go up!

You and I, hermetic
Our buttocks taut
Our carotid knotted
In the neck fiber
Our sharp feet pointing
As in spasm.

And when,
Above, there
Beyond, farther than over beyond
Farther than Betelgeuse's veil
After Altair's country
On God's brain
In a last impetus
Freed from the spirit
Stripped from the flesh
We shall possess one another.

And we shall die
We shall die high, immensely
IMMENSELY HIGH.

Death

Death comes from far off
From the end of the skies
It comes to my eyes
It will come to yours
It descends from the stars
From the white stars
From the crazy stars
Fugitives from God
It comes unforeseen
Never anticipated!
She who is in life
The great one expected:
Desperate
From the fratricidal love
Of men, oh! of men
Who kill **death**
Because they are afraid of life.

Ballad of the Red Light District

Poor gonorrhetic flowers
Who shed at night
Your poisoned petals!
You poor things, bent, withered
Orchids of shamelessness.
You are not Lelia Tenebrosa
Nor are you Vanda Tricolor:
You are fragile rickety
Dahlias cut from the stalk,

Discolored corollas
Cloistered without faith.
Ah, young whores of the evening,
What has happened
That you have poisoned the pollen
God gave you?
You still distort your faces in smiles
In your lighted cages,
Showing the red of your gums,
Speaking about things of love,
And at times you sing, howling
Like bitches at the moon
That through your nameless street
Rolls lost in the sky . . . .
But what evil glint of a star
Do I see in your lilac eyes
When you lie to young men
And make them enter!
Then I feel that in your sex
Is distilled immediately
The rotten venom
With which you poison them.
Oh, merciful women!
Sleek, broad-butted lady pimps,
Soaked in jasmine,
Throwing happy songs
Into endless perspectives.
You sing, matronly hyenas,
Songs of pandering,
You fat serene Polacks
Always ready to cry.
How you suffer, what silence
Must not be crying in you,
That immense and atrocious silence
Of the saints and of heroes.

And the counterpoint of voices
With which you enlarge the mystery,
How similar it is
To the votive lights of a cemetery
Sculptured with memories!
Poor, tragic women,
Multidimensional:
Neutral gear of chauffeurs,
Passageway of sailors!
Blonde French mulattos
Dressed for Carnaval:
Are you living the feast of flowers
Along the main deck of those streets
Tied up to the canal?
Where are your songs winging,
Where is your ship sailing?
Why do you remain motionless,
You allergic sensitive plants,
In the gardens of that hospital
Ethylic and heliotropic?
Why don't you slit your throats,
Oh, you enemies? or why don't you
Set fire to your clothes
And hurl yourselves like torches
Against those men of nothing
In that No Man's Land!

Epitaph

Here lies the Sun
Who created the dawn
And gave light to the day
And pastured the afternoon.

The magic shepherd
Of luminous hands
Who impregnated the roses
And stripped them of their petals.

Here lies the Sun
The hermaphrodite gentle
And violent, who

Possessed the shape
Of all the women
And died in the sea.

Piece

Who was it, asked the Cello,
That disobeyed me?
Who was it that entered my kingdom
And touched my gold?
Who was it that jumped over my wall
And gathered my roses?
Who was it, asked the Cello,
And the Flute answered: It was me.

But who was it, the Flute asked,
That appeared in my room?
Who was it that gave me a kiss
And slept in my bed?
Who was it that made me lost
And deceived me?
Who was it, asked the Flute,
And the old Cello smiled.

Rocking the Dead Son

Man sitting in a rocking chair
Sitting in a rocking chair
In a rocking chair
In a rocking
Rocking his dead son.

Man sitting in a rocking chair
Your entire body says yes
Your body says yes
Says yes
Yes, that your son is dead.

Man sitting in a rocking chair
Like a pendulum back and forth
The neck weak, the leg sad,
The eyes full of sand
Sand of the dead son.

Nothing will restore your son to life
Man sitting in the rocking chair
Your stockings drooping, your tie
Undone, your face unshaven:
They are the death
                they are the death
The death of the dead son.

Silence of a room: and withered flowers.
Farther, the frail cry of a woman
A cry . . . the eye open on the void
And in the silence the precise feeling
Of the voice, of the laugh, of the feeble complaint.

From the sockets the sorrowful eyes
Flee, soft, crawl like snails
After the sweet, vanished mark
Of the vomit, of the fall, of the urine.
From the arm the delirious hand flees
To caress the imponderable light
Of hair without sound and without perfume.
From the mouth the impatient lips flee
For the colorless kiss on the absent skin.
Waves of love are born and break
Against the table, the shelf, the marble stone.
There is nothing but the silence
Where with feet of ice a child
Plays, perfectly transparent
His flesh of milk, rose and talcum.
Poor father, poor, poor, poor, poor
Without memory, without muscle, without anything
But a rocking chair
In the infinite vacantness . . . grief
Gagged your mouth with bitterness
And slapped your face into paleness.
You hold in your arms a pure image
And not your son;—you are tossing
A bit of space and not your son.
It is not curls that you blow, but ashes
Stifling the air where you breathe.
Your son is dead; perhaps one day he would be
The cherished dove, the glory, the harvest
Of your future as a father; but new and tender
Angel, he was taken by death, anxious
At seeing him so small and already exhausted
With pain—and now everything is death
In you, you have no more tears, and bitter
Is the spit of the cigarette in your mouth.

But let me tell you, awe-struck man
Sitting in the rocking chair,
I who live in the abyss, I who know
The insides of the guts of women,
I who lie at night with the corpses
And deliver the dawns from my breast!
Your son is not dead! faith saves you
For the contemplation of his face
That was turned today into the little star
Of evening, into the young tree that grows
In your hand; your son is not dead!
An eternal child is being born
From the hope of a world in freedom;
They will all be your sons, just man,
Exactly like your own son; take off your tie,
Clean your dirty nails, get up, shave,
Go comfort your wife who is crying . . .
And let the rocking chair remain
In the room, now alive, rocking
The final rock of the dead son.

Christmas Poem

For this we were made:
To remember and to be remembered,
To weep and to cause tears,
To bury our dead—
That is why we have arms long for goodbyes,
Hands to pick what was given,
Fingers to dig the earth.

Such will our life be:
Always an afternoon to forget,

A star to go out in the darkness,
A path between two graves—
That is why we must have wakes,
Speak low, step softly, watch
The night sleeping in silence.

There is not much to say:
A song over a cradle,
A verse, maybe, of love,
A prayer for those who leave—
But let us not forget this hour
And for it let our hearts
Separate, solemn and simple.

Thus for this we were made:
For the hope in miracle,
For the sharing in poetry,
For looking upon the face of death—
Suddenly, we shall wait no longer . . .
Today the night is young; only from death
Are we born, immensely.

DOMINGOS CARVALHO DA SILVA

(1 9 1 5 —)

A Bit of Flame

Well I remember
what was once a street with houses
what was once a tree with branches
but I can no longer discern
a tree from a theater,
a flag from a building with windows.

Suddenly everything has changed;
I have lost the science of measuring time;
of separating and uniting things.
The hours roll like the arms of a windmill.
The events pass as confused as clouds.
The names of things are mixed up
in the salt and the sand.
The dead converse with the living
and those who are to come smile in the past
as though the rivers flowed back to their springs.

I do not look for myself in the mirror
for I am a bit of flame.
And if I seek myself like Narcissus, what I see in the water
is your face.
I close my eyelids

but your eyes walk inside them.
Your eyes are two children calling me,
inside them I walk with you hand in hand.

I hug you in your eyes, my hand rests like a leaf
on your hair
on your forehead
on your face.
We stop in your eyes under the shade of a cassia tree.
We sit on the grass and contemplate
the same section of sky.

If we had enough tears, we would bathe together
in your eyes.
We would dive into the depth of your pupils.
We would be under the sun again, stripped like a river,
and I would have the temptation of your hands.
I would kiss your cheeks as though they were
the cheeks of a rainbow.

I would show you that the whole world exists;
that an available Nature exists;
that a necessary tomorrow exists;
that there are interminable hours
in the casing of clocks
and endless water to flow
from the sides of mountains;
trees without number to spring from the earth,
arms for endless embraces,
words for measureless tenderness, the sweet tenderness
of mouths.

There are endless nights that will be born
from the seed of centuries;
endless mornings for the singing of birds.

See those roads full of dust, those fields
where orange trees exhibit their golden freckles.

I do not recognize myself any more
nor do I find myself again in the paths
lost among mimosa trees.
Your waist is as slender as the corn stalk
and your hips swing with its leaves.
I would love to hide you among the shrubs
of cotton,
to cover your body with small white flakes,
to shower on your breasts the pureness
of the earth.

And if suddenly the bells should peal
or the trumpets of Jehoshaphat should blow,
we would hide under the ooze
to triumph over Eternity.

Elegy for the Viaduct Suicides

They were already dead
in the maternal womb.
For them
the breaking dawn was already a tomb.
They fled towards death
although tied to the umbilical cord.

The sterile moon made her rounds among cypresses.
And the earth of thistles and white lilies
was joy, wheat, leprosy, tempest.
They were already dead when they were born
chained to the Civil Code.

They were given a name. What for?
They were already irrevocably dead.
Dead without the cellular spasm of the living,
they were pure clay, the immaculate mud
of swamps.

They should have gone to school—though dead—and learned
the names of statues, the dates of the eclipses,
read in the daily paper a news already dead
about remote yesterday,
believed in immortality,
they who had been dead ever since the uterine morning.

They thought at times of railroad trips.
Of ships that set sail for Constantinople.
They wanted an island uninhabited by gods,
they wanted naked women, wanted to embrace them.

But they were already dead to dream and to voyage.
Their bodies were cold water without nuptial tides.
Lifeless as trees, they had green hair
and feet furrowing the earth and hands jailing the sun.

For them suicide was merely the gesture
of a seagull settling upon an asphalt beach.
The massacred body lost only a hundred grams
of blood, of impatience, and of soul.

They were already buried with their eyes retaining
the final landscape and the ultimate disdain.
Now they have returned serene to the dark placenta
of the earth: bride, daughter,
concubine and mother.

Above their still fresh graves new plants now sprout.
Grass is growing its cover. Clover is going to blossom.

And when night falls silent and profound
it is easy to see on the tombs
the smiling faces of the suicides.

Tertiary Poem
to João Cabral de Melo Neto

Horses have once been pigeons
with wings of cloud. A river
washed the face of dawn.
Horses have once been pigeons
in the daybreak of primeval time.

Where now there are forests
once there were oblong gulfs
where tranquil fish swam.
A finders-keepers moon
traversed the night. And left
ellipses of a fire-flying
comet on the grass
of the banks, until the dawn
of the Golden Age of primeval time,
when winged horses
wore stars in their manes
as white as the plumes of a dove.

The Word did not exist.
God was not yet created.
Only the sponges were dozing
transpierced with swords
of metallic immaculate water.

And the seagulls were planning
stratospheric stops
near the Iberian shores.
And the mountains came tumbling down
in tertiary death-rattles,
in agonies of thunder,
in the mornings of Atlantic sun,
when martial squadrons of pigeons
cut the clouds
—white elegant horses.

Your hair was still moss.
Your eyes the cold body
of a half-alive oyster.
And your ever-living soul
floated on the ocean
like a lost star.

Your heart was a shell
closed and without pulsation.
And your gesture—which is your smile—
was a static mineral
not yet dug up
by the hard and phlegmatic sea.

Horses have once been pigeons.
And the silver which cats
wear on their claws glittered
in uterine vibrations
in the womb of the cold earth,
when the day was merely dawn
and God did not yet exist,
in the daybreak of primeval time.

The Pastor of Hyenas

Dawn dawn.
I will run away at dawn
with a sun in each cloud
and a moon on every road.
I will take in my hands a grate
of the cell where I locked myself.
I will run away at dawn
with you or another woman
to violate the ways
that lose themselves in the world.

I will run away at dawn
among the ships in harbor:
the pulses full of blood,
veins broken throughout the body.
I will run away from your embrace.
I will run away from your punishment.
I will hug the hyenas.
I will burn stacks of wheat.

I will be a ghost in the fields.
A dead man at the crossroads.
Only the ravens will find
my body, which you once held close . . . .
I will run away at dawn
like a merciless cyclone,
kissing the belly of waters,
as I once kissed your belly.

Dawn dawn.
Sponge that wipes out the stars.

I will run away at dawn,
shattering my chains.
I will run like a firebug
with my eyes in flames
and my upheld hand brandishing
the torch of your hair.

Message

Far, far away, a country contemplates us.
A country of silicon and gravel, of salt water and sun,
where the fish do not swim to, where the ravens settle not.
Where the shipwrecked drown in the fire
of the day solitary
and eternal.

Far, far away, where the sand reflects
the scales of the moon;
where only the dead go kiss the beach,
there we shall be one day.

In impassive caves complete vacancy will reign.
Our voice will wither like a singed
wisp of straw.

There we shall be, my love, and in wineskins of burning oil
we will enter the mineral world. And then
the earth will blossom. And from your body
will germinate gardenias and swallows,
and the world will resurrect from the abolition of death.

The Unrevealed Rose

Run about the world and seek new words for a poem.
From the oceans bring names of fish and far-off islands,
braids of virgins, drowned breasts,
dead eyelids, mutilated dreams,
but
above all, words for a poem.

Walk in darkness in quest of a rose.
Pluck from thistles the disdained flower.
Search the sea for lichens, for sponges,
bring back with you pearls,
black fish and submarine plants.

Return with the shipwrecked woman, her eyes devoured
by seagulls. The shipwrecked woman with breasts like moons
among the cypress-like seaweeds. The shipwrecked woman
with thighs like beaches
where desire spumes and faints.

Do not look for longings and tenderness
or for a singing bird in a cage.
I want you dark night, dark body
of a woman in silence, inviolable rose.

Bring back from the night words for a poem.
The unrevealed death for a poem.

Apocalypse

Because the moon is white and the night
is a mere herald of dawn;

and because the sea is just the sea
and the fountainhead does not sing or wail;

and because salt disintegrates
and roses are made of water and carbon,
and light is only a vibration
that excites nervous cells;

and because sound affects the ears
and the wind plays an Aeolian harp;
and because the earth generates asps
among poppies and magnolias;

and because the train is about to leave,
and the raven is croaking NEVERMORE;
and because we must smile
before twilight fades away;

and because yesterday no longer exists
and what is to come will come no more,
and because we are dancing a ballet
on the trigger of an H bomb:

we will not march to the Wall
of Lamentations, in order to mourn
for the frustration of everything
that we dreamed to dare, without daring.

Puppets changed into gnomes,
let us face the Apocalypse
like helmsmen in the storm
between the earthquake and the eclipse.

Let us dance on the deck
before the ship settles;

let us greet the dying sun
and the coming night, cold and eternal.

Let us laugh at this universe
reflected upon our eyes;
when we close them, the world will be
as though it had never existed.

Let us crackle among the flares
our last ecstasy;
because tomorrow we will be only
a bit of ashes in the wind.

JOÃO CABRAL DE MELO NETO

(1 9 2 0 —)

Only the Blade of a Knife

Just like a bullet
Buried in the body,
Thickening one side
Of the dead man;

Just like a bullet
Of the heaviest lead,
In the muscle of a man
Weighting it down on one side;

Like a bullet that should have
A living mechanism,
A bullet that should possess
An active heart,

Equal to that of a clock
Submerged in a body,
To that of a living clock
Which is also rebellious,

A clock that should have
The cutting edge of a knife
And all the impiety
Of a blue-tinted blade;

145

Just like a knife
That without pocket or sheath
Would turn itself into a part
Of your own anatomy;

Just like an intimate knife
Or a knife for internal use,
Inhabiting a body
Like the very skeleton

Of a man who would have one,
And always, full of pain,
Of a man who would bruise himself
Against his own proper bones.

A

Be it a bullet, a clock,
Or a furious blade,
It is nevertheless an absence
Which such a man carries.

But what is not in the man
Is just like a bullet:
It has the instrumentality of lead,
The same compact fiber.

What is not in the man
Is just like a clock
Pulsating in its cage,
Without fatigue, without indolence.

What is not in the man
Is just like the jealous

Presence of a knife,
Of any new knife.

That is why the best
Of the symbols employed
Is a cruel blade
(Even better if a Sheffield):

Because no symbol indicates
This oh so voracious absence
Like the image of a knife
Which would have only its blade,

No symbol indicates better
This avid absence
Than the image of a knife
Which has been reduced to its mouth,

Than the image of a knife
Which has been given over entirely
To hunger for the things
That are felt in knives.

    B

Among the most astonishing
Is the life of such a knife:
A knife or any metaphor
Can be cultivated.

Even more astonishing still
Is its culture:
It grows not by what it eats
But rather by how it fasts.

You can abandon it,
That internal knife:
You will never find it
With an empty mouth.

Out of nothing it distills
Acidity and vinegar
And other strategems
Peculiar to sabers.

And like the knife it is,
Vehement and dynamic,
It makes its perverse mechanism
Go off without any help:

The naked blade
Which grows as it wears,
Which the less it sleeps
The less sleep there is,

Which the more it cuts
The more it increases its cutting edge
And keeps on giving birth
To others, like a spring.

(For the life of such a knife
Is measured in reverse:
Be it a clock or a bullet,
Or be it the knife itself.)

C

Be careful with the object,
With the object be careful,

Even though it is only a bullet
Of that molded lead,

Because the teeth
Of the bullet are already blunt
And very easily become
More blunt in the muscle.

Be much more careful
When it is a clock,
With its heart
Burning and spasmodic.

Be especially careful
Or the pulse of the clock
And the pulse of the blood
Will keep the same time,

Or its copper so neat
Will mistake its pace
For the blood which beats
Without biting any longer.

And if it is the knife,
Be even more careful:
The sheath of the body
May absorb the steel.

Sometimes also its edge
Tends to become hoarse
And there are cases in which blades
Degenerate into leather.

The important thing is for the knife
Not to lose its passion

And for the wooden handle
Not to corrupt it.

D

And sometimes this knife
Turns itself off
And that's what is called
The low tide of the knife.

Maybe it does not turn itself off,
Maybe it has only fallen asleep.
If the image is a clock,
Its bee ceases to buzz.

But whether it sleeps or turns itself off:
When such an engine stops,
The entire soul acquires
An alkaline quality

Quite similar to the neutral
Substance, very much like felt,
Which is that of the souls
Who do not have skeleton-knives.

And the sword of this blade,
Its flame flickering before,
And the nervous clock
And that indigestible bullet,

All of them follow the process
Of the blade that blinds:
They become knife, clock,
Or bullet of wood,

Bullet of leather or cloth,
Or clock of coal tar,
They become a knife without backbone,
A knife of clay or of honey.

(But when you no longer wait
For the tide,
Here is the knife resurging
With all its crystals.)

E

It is necessary to keep
The knife well hidden
Because in the dampness
Its flash doesn't last long.

(In dampness created by
The spit of conversation,
The more intimate it is
The muddier it gets.)

This care is necessary
Even if the live coal
That inhabits you is not a knife
But is a clock or a bullet.

For they cannot stand
All the weathers:
Their wild flesh
Demands Spartan quarters.

But if you must remove them
In order to suffer them stronger,
Let it be in some desert
Or wilderness in the open air.

But never let it be in air
Visited by birds.
It must be a severe air
Without shade and without vertigo.

And let it never be at night,
For the night has fertile hands.
Let it be in the acids of the sun,
The acids of the Equatorial sun,

Let it be in the fever of this sun
That turns the grass into wire,
That makes a sponge of the wind
And that molds the earth into thirst.

F

Whether it is that bullet
Or any other image,
Whether even a clock is
The wound that keeps,

Or even a knife
That would have only its blade,
Of all images
The most voracious and graphic,

No man will be able
To remove it from his body,
Whether it be a bullet
Or a clock or a knife,

Nor does it matter
The radius of its blade:
Whether a tame table knife,
Or the ferocious Bowie.

And if he who suffers its rape
Is unable to remove it,
Even less can the hand
Of a neighbor pull that knife out.

The entire medicine
Of numeral knives
And arithmetical tweezers
Can do nothing against it.

Neither can the police
With all their surgeons,
Nor can time itself
With all its bandages.

Nor can the hand of him
Who unwittingly has planted
Bullet, clock, or knife,
Images of fury.

G

This bullet that a man
Carries at times in his flesh
Makes all those who keep it
Less rarefied.

What this clock implies
For recalcitrant and insect:
Cloistered in the body,
It makes this more alert.

And if the metaphor is a knife
Of him who carries it in his muscle,

Knives inside a man
Give him a greater impulse.

The cutting edge of a knife
Biting a human body
Arms that body
With another knife or dagger,

For by keeping alive
All the springs of the soul,
It gives the impetus of a blade
And the mating time of cutlery,

Besides having the constricted body
That keeps the knife
Insoluble in sleep
And in everything vague,

As in that story,
Told by someone,
Of a man who fashioned himself
A memory so precise

That he could preserve
For thirteen years in the palm of his hand
The feminine weight
Of a farewell clasp.

H

When he who suffers the symbols
Works with words,
The clock, the bullet, and the knife
Are useful to him.

Men who in general
Work at this trade
Have in the storehouse
Only extinct words:

Some that suffocate
Under the dust,
Others that are unseen
Among the big knots;

Words that have lost
Through wear all their metal
And the sand which retains
The attention that reads badly.

For only this knife
Will give such a worker
Eyes more fresh
For his vocabulary

And only this knife
And the example of its tooth
Will teach him to obtain
From sick material

That which in all knives
Is their best quality:
The ferocious acuteness,
A certain electricity,

Plus the keen violence
That they have in such precision,
The taste of desert,
—The style of knives!

I

This enemy blade,
This clock or bullet,
If it makes more alert
All those who keep it,

It also knows how to awaken
The objects around it
And even the very liquids
Can acquire bones.

And all that was vague,
All the loose matter,
For him who suffers the knife
Assumes nerves, jagged points.

Everything around it
Takes on a more intense life,
With the sharpness of a needle
And the attitude of a wasp.

In everything the side
Which cuts reveals itself,
And they who looked
As round as wax

Now strip themselves
From the mists of routine,
They begin to function
With all their corners.

For among so many things
That do not sleep any longer,

The man whom the knife cuts
And to whom it lends its edge,

Suffering that blade
And its thrust so cold,
He passes, lucid and sleepless,
He goes, cutting edge against cutting edge.

*　　*　　*

Returning from that knife,
Friend or enemy,
Which compresses a man
The more it chews him;

Returning from that knife
Which a man carries so secretly
And which must be carried
Like the hidden skeleton;

From the image where I stayed
The longest, the image of the blade,
Because of all the images
It is certainly the most voracious;

For returning from the knife
One goes up to the other image,
That of the clock
Biting under the flesh,

And from it to the other,
The first, that of the bullet,
Which has a thick tooth
But a strong stride,

And from there to the memory
That clothed such images
And is much more intense
Than was the power of language,

And finally to the presence
Of reality, the first,
Which created the memory
And still creates it, still.

At last to reality,
The first and of such violence
That in trying to apprehend it
Every image shatters.

PAULO BOMFIM

(1 9 2 7 —)

Tempest

The tempest lives
As though you were the man walking through it
The tempest lives
As though you were
Rain, wind and lightning
Walking through the man.

The Sea

By way of the bridge of spume
You have arrived.
I don't know beyond the beach:
The world that generated you;
Whether you have sprung from the breast of day
Or from the cry of night.
I recognize myself only
In the coral of fingernails and of mouth,
In the liquid eyes,
In the braids of seaweed.
I know that you float in me,

And your body is clothed
In voices;
Yet
You will return to the world of white sands,
And my whisper will be salt,
Shining in your hair.

The Fourth Kingdom

Your hair will tell you
Of the soul of the forest,
Your teeth will reflect
The language of rocks,
Your body will cry
The hunger of animals.
You will be rescued from the shipwreck
Of red rivers:
Forget the cradle of light
And turn yourself into light.

Hands

My stranger hands
Darning the non-being,
Gathering silver bluebells
In empty flowerbeds,
Caressing faces
That smile sweetly
With the melancholy of everything that will not exist.
My stranger hands,
Crossed in the night,
Do not recognize themselves.

Reincarnation

I die with the days.
Each night is a trip
Through the kingdom of the dead,
A flower that dispetals
On my bloodless fingers,
A life that I lose
Among angles of fire.
Each morning I keep silent
Before what I was,
I discover the sun for the first time,
And I let the flesh envelop
The mystery of the bones,
And the bones bear on their white stems
Buds of eternity.

Madness

To sow poppies
In the gardens of chance.
To be delirium with kindled feet,
Tracing spirals
In humid tunnels of brilliance.
To feel yourself as laughter of mirrors,
Music of daggers,
Forest lost in fear.
To grope
In the chasm that attracts chasms,
In the moons of nothing dreaming transparencies,
In silver bells burnt with sound.
To be the gardens of chance,
The sick nerves,

The ruined wall of the captured world;
To die with the cry
And to be reborn from the monochord idea
That drips in the soul
Of the great glassy-eyed day.

The Shadow

We were planned
To deny.
We were created
To be
The night before the star.
We are the black angel
That visits the flesh:
In us the colors are perfumes,
Drops of sun
That slowly evaporate
After moistening the face of the dead.
We inhabit the interior of forms,
The emptiness of gestures,
The solitude of life.
In the night of ages we kindled the torch of gold
So that men would find themselves reflected.
Denying, we affirm.
In the noon of ages
We are soul.

The Idea

He who dies
Turns into idea.

Think your dead.
In each word
Two eyes are spying upon you from the past.
Everything sleeps in the depth of us:
The dispetaled roses in the gardens of Persia,
The moons of blood in Babylon,
The silver galleys sinking in the Nile.
What passes
Remains.
One day we shall be ideas
Fructifying silence.
Then, no one will remember us
Because we will be present,
In the soul of the idea, in the spoken flesh.

The Invention

Invent in the undergrounds
Moist with silence
The life that created you.
Change the idea into flesh,
The thought into rock,
The dream into water,
The anxiety into fire,
The death into cloud.
Recreate the form
That surrounds you:
Return to the elements that make your flesh,
Return to the beginning of your mystery:
You will be the stone-tomb,
The wood-coffin,
The undone rose,

The male and the female,
Good and evil.
From the womb of your grief
You will be reborn,
Bent over yourself
You will suck the night
And from your lips the day will flow.
—Invent death.

BIOGRAPHICAL NOTES

MANUEL BANDEIRA

Born in Recife, Pernambuco, on April 19, 1886, Manuel Bandeira has evoked his childhood memories of that Venice of Brazil for the production of some of his finest elegies. Unable to become an architect, as his father wanted him to be, because of the tuberculosis which poisoned his youth and handicapped most of his adult life, Bandeira wrote poetry, in his own phrase, "like one who dies" and became what he describes as a "minor poet." Bandeira's humility, however, cannot hide the fact that he is one of the greatest lyric voices in the history of the Portuguese language. His works were recognized as modern classics in Brazil by the time he was fifty; today at seventy-five Manuel Bandeira enjoys the best health of his life, membership in the Brazilian Academy of Letters, and immense personal fame and influence. Something of a national institution in Brazil, he holds in his native land a literary position similar to that of T. S. Eliot in England and Robert Frost in the United States. Bandeira's major poetic works, all published in Rio de Janeiro, his beloved adopted city, include: *A Cinza das Moras* (1917); *Carnaval* (1919); *Poesias* (1924); *Libertinagem* (1930); *Estrêla da Manhã* (1936); *Poesias Completas* (1940, 1945, 1947). Bandeira's own critical account of his development as a poet may be found in his *Itinerário de Pasárgada* (1954).

MARIO DE ANDRADE

Mario Raul de Morais Andrade, born in the city of São Paulo on October 9, 1893, was a perfect example of the ethnic trinity of

Brazil: he was a mixture of Indian, Negro, and Portuguese. His multi-racial stock served as a symbol of his multiform genius, the most varied in the history of Brazilian literature. His complete works run to nineteen thick volumes: poetry, short stories, novels; critical writings on literature, folklore, music, dramatic dances, and the plastic arts; literary theory, general aesthetics, philology, and linguistics. From his entrance into the Modernist Movement in Brazil about 1920 until his death in 1945, Andrade sought to create a pragmatic aesthetic; above all else, he wanted his writing to be useful. As a national catalytic agent and professor at large, he opposed the old classical concepts of beauty, order, proportion and harmony. For him these artistic values are not frozen ideograms but warm and living ideas in constant motion and change. If a spirit of destructive experimentalism vitiates the quality of much of Andrade's work, his overall influence on Brazilian culture has been larger than that of anyone else in the twentieth century.

JORGE DE LIMA

A simple man, described as kindness itself by his friends, the many-faceted mulatto from the Northeast, Jorge de Lima, was the most versatile of all modern Brazilian poets. Born in União, Alagoas, on April 23, 1893, Lima became, after a brief period of fame as a neo-Parnassian, the chief representative of lyric poetry within the Northeast Regionalist Movement. A folkloric genius who could recite a vast store of tales, he nourished his natural love for all things animate and inanimate, and developed in time a super-natural charity based upon a Christian mysticism that permitted him to see the universe in the eternal sacrifice of Calvary. Celebrating the Negro as no other Brazilian poet has been able to do and creating fantastic visions that troubled his imagination and often kept him from sleep, Jorge de Lima also wrote neo-naturalistic novels and surrealistic prose. But so great was his poetic achievement that Brazilian criticism still finds it difficult to decide which part of his work deserves the greatest admiration: his Christian or his regional poetry. Lima's later volumes are his most impressive: *Tempo e Eternidade* (in collaboration with Murilo Mendes, 1935); *A Túnica Inconsútil* (1938); *Poemas Negros* (1946); *Livro de Sonetos* (1949); *Invenção de Orfeu* (1952).

CASSIANO RICARDO

Born in São José dos Campos, São Paulo, on July 26, 1895, Cassiano Ricardo Leite was a member of the Green-and-Yellow Group of the Modernist Movement in Brazil. Opposed to the kind of primitivism championed by Oswald de Andrade, Ricardo favored the study of Indian contributions to the structure of Brazilian civilization and wanted to give art a social and political function. Turning from his early Parnassian verse and his combative Modernist volumes, Cassiano matured into a poet of the primitive land, of the subjective world of the self, where with a profusion of images his best poems remain—in the words of Manuel Bandeira—"like snapshots taken under the raw light of mid-day." As a nationalist who has constantly stood against all racial and cultural preconceptions and who has fought against negativism, irony, and despair in his country's literature, Cassiano Ricardo has seen his reputation rise steadily in Brazilian criticism. His collected poetry (1947) filled three substantial volumes.

CECILIA MEIRELES

At the foot of Corcovado Mountain in Rio de Janeiro, where an electric cable train leaves every hour with sightseers bound for the base of the great Christ statue, Cecilia Meireles lives with her husband Meitor Grillo in a comfortable two-story home. Born a Carioca on November 7, 1901, by the time of the first phase of the Modernist Movement in Brazil, she already belonged to the Spiritualists, a group of writers who were direct descendants of the Symbolists of Paraná. Friend of the Chilean Nobel laureate Gabriela Mistral, Cecilia Meireles has constantly fostered two aesthetic forces in her poetry: tradition and mystery. Perhaps the most dedicated craftsman of her generation, greatly admired in India, Israel, and the Latin countries of Western Europe, she has created a dozen volumes of lyrics so limpid and intense as to be the envy of her male contemporaries. These volumes, collected in *Obra Poética* (1958), run to better than a thousand pages. The union of such quantity with such quality is one reason why she has twice been nominated for the Nobel Prize. Despite her many honors, she is happiest when performing little acts of kindness for her husband, three daughters, and five grandchildren.

CARLOS DRUMMOND DE ANDRADE

An archivist at the Ministry of Education in Rio de Janeiro, Carlos Drummond de Andrade has provoked more passionate discussion and a wider range of differing interpretations than any other modern poet in Brazil. Certainly the most important voice in the second phase of the Modernist Movement in Brazil, and perhaps the greatest living poet in South America at this time, Carlos Drummond was born in Itabira, Minas Gerais, October 31, 1902. Alienated, as he himself admits, from "everything in life that is open and talkative," Drummond is hard as diamond in his sarcasm and irony: that is the Mineiro in him. Economical of means, he perseveres to heroic ends: that is his Scottish ancestry. He is grateful for little things, wants to live and love "without mystification": that is the Carioca he would like to become. After a generation of constant literary growth, Drummond has achieved in his poetry a perfect fusion of sensibility and reason: that is the history of his genius. Nowhere can that history be better read than in *Poemas*, a collection of the nine volumes of poetry that he had published before 1959.

MURILO MENDES

Born in Juiz de Fera, Minas Gerais, on May 13, 1902, Murilo Monteiro Mendes thinks of his poems as studies that other men can develop, because he believes that "the germ of poetry exists in all men." For the growth of that germ in himself, Mendes credits three events as primary in importance: the passage of Halley's Comet in 1910, two Russian ballets featuring Nijinsky in 1916, and his own meeting with Ismael Nery in 1921. He attributes to the comet the qualities of panic and sharp clarity that characterize his poetry, and also the two planes of vision; the ballets induced a kind of dancing quality in his rhythms; the meeting with Nery led to Murilo's conversion to Catholicism. The influence of Nery's Catholic Essentialism upon Murilo Mendes' poetry may be seen in his abstraction of space and time, his incorporation of the eternal into the contingent. Dialectical in both his poetry and his religion, Mendes came to believe that the essence of truth is Christian love, divine charity. His spiritual voice speaks most movingly perhaps in the following volumes: *A Poesia em Pânico* (1938), *O Visionario* (1941), *As Metamorfoses* (1944), *Mundo Enígma* (1945), and *Poesia Liberdade* (1947).

AUGUSTO FREDERICO SCHMIDT

As Economic Adviser in the Administration of President Juscelino Kubitschek (1956-61), Ambassador Augusto Frederico Schmidt, who was born in Rio de Janeiro, April 20, 1906, was partially responsible for the political planning that led to the development of the Organization of American States. His prophetic fear of the Communist overthrow of democratic governments in underdeveloped Latin America has, in turn, had direct bearing upon the decision of President Kennedy to launch the Alliance For Progress. As a poet, after his early work in Romanticism, Schmidt found that he had a certain affinity with the French religious poet who lost his life in World War I—Charles Péguy. As a consequence of this affinity, in the words of Manuel Bandeira, Schmidt "passed through the Modernist experience, profited from some of its lessons, and separated from it by expressing himself in a constantly serious and grave tone, like a Biblical prophet." It is, in short, the return to the sublime that constitutes the primary quality of Schmidt's poetry, a quality demonstrated in *Navio Perdido* (1929), *Pássaro Cego* (1930), *Canto da Noite* (1934), *A Estrêla Solitária* (1940), *Mar Desconhecido* (1942), *O Galo Branco* (1948), and *Fonte Invisível* (1949).

VINICIUS DE MORAIS

Undoubtedly the most Bohemian of all modern Brazilian poets, Vinicius de Melo Morais was born in Rio de Janeiro on October 19, 1913. A diplomat by profession—he has had extended tours of duty in such places as Los Angeles, Paris, and Montevideo—Morais is celebrated in Brazil for his mastery of lyrics for the samba and the popular song. His serious poetry reflects an obsession with the constant warfare between the flesh and the spirit. In both his person and his poetry, he has waged a continual struggle to resolve, in the words of the Carioca novelist Otávio de

Faria, that perplexity which exists between "the impossible purity and the inacceptable impurity." Looking upon himself as a combination of Romeo and the Three Musketeers, Morais has nevertheless maintained a severity in his art that has expunged prosaic expressions, invested regular meters with the vitality of colloquial, enriched rhythms, and returned to strength and economy of form. In *Novos Poemas* (1938), for example, he wrote some of the finest sonnets in Brazilian literature; some of his visual patterns in *Cinco Elegias* (1943), on the other hand, mark him as an immediate forerunner of Concretism. As of 1959, his poetic output ran to twelve volumes.

DOMINGOS CARVALHO DA SILVA

Born in Vila Nova de Gaia, Portugual, in 1915, Domingos Carvalho da Silva came to Brazil with his parents and took up residence in São Paulo in 1924; in 1937 he became a naturalized Brazilian citizen. A kind of adopted member of the Generation of 1945, he possesses an immense capacity for work. In addition to his published translations from the poetry of Pablo Neruda (1946), his several volumes of prose, his countless critical articles in *O Estado de São Paulo, Diário de São Paulo, Anhembi,* and many other leading Brazilian journals and newspapers, Silva has published seven important volumes of his own poetry: *Bem-Amada Ifigênia* (1943), *Rosa Extinta* (1945), *Praia Oculta* (1949), *O Livro de Lourdes* (1952), *Girassol de Outono* (1952), *Poemas Escolhidos* (1956), and *Fênix Refratária* (1959). In his best poetry, Silva portrays the oceanic origins of life. Master of the weird and haunting image, he believes in the immortality of the basic elements and in man's personal resurrection from the mineral world into higher forms of life.

JOÃO CABRAL DE MELO NETO

The undisputed leader of the Generation of 1945 is poet-diplomat João Cabral de Melo Neto. Like Manuel Bandeira before him, Melo Neto was born in Recife in 1920. Recently returned· to Brazil from a long and pleasant tour of duty as secretary of his nation's embassy in Madrid, Melo Neto has, according to Vinicius de Morais, "discovered woman in his latest poetry." Famous for his intellectual asceticism, he has continually changed his conception of poetry. In *Pedra do Sono* (1942), for example, poetry is sleep and dream and hallucination and the free play of words. In *O Engenheiro* (1945), poetry becomes a rigid construction in which there is neither revelation nor inspiration, but reasoning for the sake of reasoning. Abandoning most of his earlier taboos, in *Psicologia da Composição* (1947) Melo Neto analyzes his own creative process, his natural habits of thought and feeling. By 1950, in his *O Cão sem Plumas*, he returns to classical tactics, in which inspiration demands rational content, the outline of thesis and affirmation. In the four volumes of poetry published since 1950, he has established himself as the leading poet of his age in Brazil.

PAULO BOMFIM

Born in São Paulo in 1927, Paulo Bomfim has become a popular cultural figure on radio and television in his native city, through his acting and recorded poetry readings. A leader of the *Diálogo* literary group, he was honored by the Brazilian Academy of Letters for his *Antônio Triste* (1946). Among his subsequent volumes of poetry, more exciting for their promise rather than for their absolute artistic worth, are *Tansfiguração* (1951), *Relógio de Sol* (1952), and *O Colecionador de Minutos* (1960).